Israel Houghton brings to worship a freshness and way of approaching God that transcends cultural distinctions, bringing God's people into His presence with an impact that is masterful. Let's follow him into the Holies of Holies with this new informative and inspirational book.

—*Bishop T. D. Jakes*
Senior Pastor, The Potter's House • Dallas, Texas

I was able to see first hand the dedication and passion of Israel and his incredible team. Through much prayer and fasting, they collectively recorded a masterpiece and wrote this book. The heart they display toward the broken is explained in song and in print with true sincerity. May God break our hearts for the things that break His as we journey through this book together.

—*Darlene Zschech*
Worship Leader, Hillsong Church • Sydney, Australia

Riveting and refreshing. These words will immediately resonate with you after being blessed by Israel Houghton's new book, *A Deeper Level*. With an amazingly transparent and vulnerable spirit, Israel has tapped into the very heart of God and leads us on a journey of true worship. Allow God to draw you closer to Him, as one of the most God-centered, God-led, and God-ordained worship leaders of our time ministers to you through the pages of *A Deeper Level*.

—*Bishop Eddie L. Long*
Senior Pastor, New Birth Missionary Baptist Church • Lithonia, Georgia

ynah Dadivas

ISRAEL HOUGHTON

A DEEPER LEVEL

WHITAKER
HOUSE

Photo credits: Live photography by Bill Starling and Sam Noerr. Photographs on pages 14, 30, 82, 124, 142, and photos with an asterisk (*) on pages 155 and 156 by ColemanArt Photography (www.ColemanArtPhotography.com)

A Deeper Level

ISBN-13: 978-0-88368-804-5
ISBN-10: 0-88368-804-2
Printed in the United States of America
© 2007 by Israel Houghton

Whitaker House
1030 Hunt Valley Circle
New Kensington, PA 15068
www.whitakerhouse.com

Library of Congress Cataloging-in-Publication Data

Houghton, Israel.
A deeper level / Israel Houghton.
p.   cm.
Summary: "Grammy Award-winning worship artist Israel Houghton discusses a lifestyle of worship from the point of living in the constant presence of God and caring about the things that He cares about"—Provided by publisher.
ISBN 978-0-88368-804-5 (trade pbk. : alk. paper) 1. Worship. I. Title.
BV10.3.I87 2007
248.3—dc22   2007025172

1 2 3 4 5 6 7 8 9 10 11 12 **UJ** 5 14 13 12 11 10 09 08 07

Dedication

To my father, Pastor Henry Houghton, and to all of the fathers of the Gospel in my life who have helped me to become a father myself.

ACKNOWLEDGMENTS

Thanks be to God for who He is and all He has done.

- Many thanks to Bob, Denise, Tom, and the entire team at Whitaker House for leading me to believe I could write the first of many books. Thank you for your belief.

- To my wife Meleasa, my Queen and my primary ministry, and our three wonderful children, Mariah, Israel Duncan, and Milan Lillie, for endless inspiration. Love you.

- To my spiritual father, Bishop Joseph Garlington: Fifteen years ago I told a friend that I felt you were the blueprint for my life, and you have truly led the way for Meleasa and me. I thank you for your love, wisdom, and example.

- Thank you to Pastor Joel Osteen for trusting me, believing in me, and writing the foreword for this book. I am so humbled.

- To New Breed: It is such a pleasure to serve you and lead you. You are not a group but a movement. Thank you for the community effort and conversational tone that you all contributed to this literary effort. Your dedication to fasting, praying, and documenting our preparation for the "Deeper" is appreciated and greatly respected.

- To Jennifer Houghton, the ultimate executive, and to Chad Dutcher, the consummate PA: I literally could do nothing without the two of you.

- Lastly, I want to acknowledge all of the worship leaders and musicians who give to the Lord and His people week after week. Keep going deeper into the presence of God.

–Israel Houghton

TABLE OF CONTENTS

foreword

BY JOEL OSTEEN

The most valuable treasures in life are found by digging deep. People invest countless amounts of time searching for diamonds, oil, and treasures of all kinds. Do you know there are treasures deep inside of you? Psalm 42:7 tells us that *"Deep calls to deep."* I believe this is referring to the depths of God's heart calling out to the depths of your heart. It is a wise person who takes the time to search for the God-given treasures within.

It's interesting that in God's kingdom, the key to having more—more of God's presence, more of His peace, more of His glory—isn't found in doing more. It's actually found in doing less. Experiencing more of God in your life is found by removing the daily distractions, and opening your heart and mind to the power of His Holy Spirit. By allowing Him to do a deep work in your heart, you will experience a deep life transformation.

Israel Houghton has been a dear friend and minister at Lakewood Church for many years. He has been a tremendous blessing to this ministry and to me personally. I know his impact is a result of His willingness to go deep with God. I've watched the fruit of his life grow as he inspires so many to go deeper in their walk with the Lord. His songs have given voice to the passion and heartbeat of this ministry, and many others around the world. He is truly a gifted musician, but more importantly, he is an experienced worshipper.

When I think of Israel's book, *A Deeper Level*, I think of a treasure map, a guide to the treasures inside your own heart. Israel's style in this book is so personal and transparent that it's like he's sitting in the room with you, encouraging you in your own journey. I know you will be blessed and strengthened by the message and stories Israel shares from his own personal journey. I encourage you, as you read these pages, to open your heart and allow the Lord to truly take you to *A Deeper Level*.

–Joel Osteen
Best-selling Author &
Senior Pastor, Lakewood Church • Houston, Texas

Identity

You are my Father
You are my Father
You hold my future and destiny
You are my Father
You are my Father
In You I find my identity

Lay Your hands on me
Tell me who I am
I can do all things
If You say I can
Show me I am free
Free to accomplish Your plan for me

—by Israel Houghton and Neville Diedericks
© 2007 Integrity's Praise! Music and Sound of the New Breed (adm
by Integrity's Praise! Music)

A New Thing

*[Jesus] said to Simon, "Now go out
where it is **deeper**
and let down your nets
and you will catch a lot of fish!"*
—Luke 5:4 (TLB, emphasis added)

Every once in a while you get a feeling that something big is about to happen.

You can't plan it. You can't force it. In the end, it isn't because of you anyway. You're just sitting there in your boat, doing what you've always done, when Jesus turns and says, *"Now go out where it is deeper."*

And something inside tells you that history is about to be made.

Sometime last year, I began work on a new CD along with my band, New Breed. It was the first recording project in which we had the concept before we had the songs. We knew it would be about going to a deeper level with God. That was the calling. To accomplish this, the first thing I started to do was to define what deeper meant.

To me, deeper meant an even more intense encounter with some of my core values, including a passion to be more cross-cultural, cross-generational, and cross-denominational. These concepts were just starting to intensify. The deeper I ventured—the further I journeyed into the presence of God—the more vivid it all became.

One thing became immediately clear: I didn't want to tell the body of Christ to go to a deeper level unless I was willing to go there myself. So, I pondered over what deeper would mean for me and for New Breed. We kicked the topic around in loose discussion for a few days. Then, when it was all said and done, I told everybody, "In a couple of days, I'm going to present something to you guys, and we are *all* going to feel this one."

What God laid on my heart was a path that He wanted us to venture down together, and part of the journey was going to entail a fast.

A Consecration

The path we were taking was going to be more than just a trial run at spiritual disciplines or a Bible study. The word we used for this journey was *consecration*. By definition, it means "to make or declare sacred; to devote irrevocably to the worship of God...to devote to a purpose with deep solemnity or dedication."

In Scripture, God said, *"You shall consecrate* **yourselves** *therefore and be holy, for I am the* LORD *your God"* (Leviticus 20:7 NASB, emphasis added). Notice, it says that this is a process that *we* do—not God. It is also something that He commands. *"Consecrate yourselves...for I am the LORD your God." "Be holy,"* be separate, be set apart, *"for I am the LORD your God."*

This consecration was going to be a period of time devoted to setting ourselves apart—apart from distraction, apart from certain foods, apart from the things of this world that vie for our time—in order to go before the Lord, fully prepared to be used by Him.

Let me say right here that this was God's intention for us. It was not out of a feeling that we were anything special. On the contrary, it was out of the knowledge that God chooses *"the foolish things of the world to shame the wise...the weak things of the world to shame the strong"* (1 Corinthians 1:27). We knew that God has a tendency to call out ordinary people to carry out His will. He does this in order to make it obvious to all that the glory is His alone. God is not looking for successful musicians or authors or pastors to carry out His will. He is looking for ordinary people who will deny themselves and consecrate themselves to be used by Him.

Therefore, if it can happen for us, it can certainly happen for you!

<u>Fasting</u>

There is great power and spiritual benefit to a fast. Jesus fasted (see Matthew 4:2), as did the early church (see Acts 13:2). Numerous heroes of the Old Testament also practiced fasting.

But there is also a problem with some fasts. They are intended to reduce your dependence on the physical as they intensify your spiritual desires and senses. But what they can become is a legalistic regimen that is more about strict *dos* and *don'ts* than about focusing on the things of God and the Holy Spirit. I didn't want this to become just about rules. When people focus on the regulations, it just makes them want to start looking for loopholes. For instance, if you've ever been on a liquid-only fast, don't tell me that you didn't dream of trying to liquefy a cheeseburger in the blender to stay within the guidelines. I know I have. When we do things under obligation, we tend to look for any way we can push the envelope.

The important thing was that we be unified in an expectation that God wanted to do something new in us, in the body of Christ, and in the Christian music industry that we represent.

The Baseline Commitment

I knew that a strict fast was not going to work for everybody. We were not going to be spending our time in a monastery praying and meditating. We were busy people. We were working musicians, traveling and practicing and keeping all the weird hours that musicians must keep. But many of us were also moms and dads with families to love and lead and provide for. In addition, we were geographically dispersed across the country and around the globe. Some of our members are as far away as South Africa!

The one constant we kept coming back to, however, was this call to strip away the obvious distractions of life that we felt got in the way of a deeper relationship with God. So we set up a baseline of participation to which we could all commit. I presented a menu of opportunities that focused on three areas of our lives: media, food, and time. We were unified that these three areas were the ones that we would address. We came up with some basic, bottom-line commitments, and then members of the group were free to go beyond the minimum in whatever way God would lead.

I introduced it to New Breed by saying, "What would happen if..."

MEDIA

The first was a media fast. We all committed not to see any movies for forty days. We decided to limit our television viewing to a strictly enforced six hours per week.

What would happen if the time we spent in these activities were spent in the Word of God, in prayer, or with actual human beings?

DIET

In the area of food, we decided that there would be no sugar, no fried food, and no soda. If we were going to drink juice, it was not to be the kind that only contains 3 percent juice. It was going to be the natural kind. The goal was to commit to living a healthier lifestyle.

What would happen if, by living healthier, we were better able to get into the presence of God, to set aside time for devotions, and to focus on the things of the spirit rather than the appetites of the flesh?

TIME

We talked about the ways in which we spent the hours of our day. What takes up the biggest chunks of our time? For me, it was entertainment and being on the phone.

What really led me to that realization was the television show *24*. When we went to Australia last year, I bought season five on DVD and watched it during the entire flight back to the US. When we landed in Los Angeles, I was watching the last episode, and I was overwhelmed with the thought: *You just spent around nineteen hours watching television in two sittings. What is your problem?*

It was strange. I realized I had the ability to completely turn my brain off and let the TV wash over me for nineteen hours. Then I thought, *What if I got into the Word of God for nineteen hours straight?*

Again, heavy-handed legalism and condemnation has never been our thing. But as a group, we have this current understanding that we are affecting a generation. Children and teenagers are watching us closely, and they are smarter than you think. They see everything! Therefore, the things we do, the things we say, the things we give ourselves to will have ripple effects for a long time. What are we doing with these moments?

That's when I decided to challenge the group by saying, "Let's cut our television time way down." I knew the Grammy Awards and the Super Bowl were during this time, so we had to plan ahead and save up our time to watch the things we really wanted to watch.

What would happen if we were able to evaluate and reprioritize the way we spent our time so we had more room in our lives for Scripture, prayer, and meditation?

What would happen if...

This was the framework of our period of consecration. We set aside a forty-day period, at which time we would go into rehearsals for the CD. The number of days is not important. Forty days was simply the period of time that we chose for our consecration. What is important is that God leads you through the process. Within the parameters we set up, people were free to go as far as they wanted to go. Some went hardcore at the spiritual disciplines. A few of our folks from South Africa decided to go ten days with just water. Others knew it was going to be a struggle just to eat a healthy diet and limit the distractions.

Staying Connected

When I presented this idea to the team, I told them that, even though we were all over the globe, we needed to stay connected. It was going to be tough, but we needed the fellowship, encouragement, and support of the team. We had to take advantage of the best technologies. So we set up a conference call each day at 11 a.m. (Central time), and everybody would be present on that call in order to pray for one another.

In addition, we used E-mail to encourage each other with daily devotions and prayers. I wrote some messages, but most were generated by the members of New Breed.

What I found incredible was the unity we experienced as we came together. We were already a pretty close-knit team, but this was different. We came together each day with prayer and fasting, challenging and encouraging each other—and our lives were changed.

I am so proud of New Breed and the way they responded to this challenge. The heart of our team was unified behind the idea that we were going to do this thing together. We all had the desire to go deeper, and we were prepared to do whatever it took to get there.

I know there are other groups out there who have been through similar experiences, but we had a feeling that God was going to take us to a place where we had never been before. We had a feeling that history was about to be made.

Accordingly, we felt that this needed to be documented in some way. Not just for us, but also for people out there who, like us, felt the need to go in a different direction—who desired to go deeper. So I asked the members of my team to keep a journal of their experiences, struggles, lessons, and breakthroughs. Since each of their journeys were different, each of their observations and experiences became a crucial part of where God was taking us and what He was doing.

Therefore, I am including their experiences and reactions throughout this book. Each entry will appear with their name, hometown, and the role they play in New Breed so you can get to know them as they join in our conversation. My prayer is that this book becomes more like a group discussion than me talking down to you from some mountaintop. I hope that, in some small way, you will get to know New Breed and feel encouraged by a connection to other believers who also desire to go deeper.

Join Us In This Consecration

This is not intended to be a book about fasting, spiritual disciplines, or avoiding the "evils" of technology and media. It is, however, about a group of ordinary people who desired to go on a journey that would take us to a deeper level with God. It is about looking at your life and deciding, for a period of time, to consecrate it to the Lord. It is about declaring your life sacred and devoting yourself, irrevocably, to the worship of God. Doing that, however, will take you to places you've never been. It will force you to make some changes in your life, at least for a season.

As I said, we are busy people with families, jobs, and responsibilities. We are not celebrities with personal assistants. If we can do this, you can do it. Won't you come with us on this journey of consecration? I implore you not to read this book just as an intellectual exercise. Dare to dive in and go deeper with us as, together, we discover things we never knew were possible.

If you are going through this book as a group, I would encourage you to pair off into partnerships for prayer, support, encouragement, and accountability. There is great power in community.

If you are going through this book as an individual, I would still encourage you to find a close friend or spiritual mentor with whom you can share your intentions. Let them know what you are trying to do. Give them permission to ask you about your progress and to hold you accountable to your desire to go deeper. Several members of New Breed have shared that, without the group dynamic of our consecration, they would not have been able to make it through.

Either way, I have left some room at the end of each chapter for you to share your desires, thoughts, and prayers. Use this to continue the conversation between you and God in which you begin to consecrate your mind, actions, and heart for His glory and worship.

Taking Inventory

To begin, I would encourage you to take some time and turn your focus inward. Let the Holy Spirit inspect the condition of your heart. There is grace in God to purge us, and then elevate us.

> *Search me, O God, and know my heart; test me and know my anxious thoughts. See if there is any offensive way in me, and lead me in the way everlasting.* (Psalm 139:23–24)

Examine yourself in regard to your relationship with God. Allow Him to expose areas of your heart that need to be surrendered or released to Him. Are there any areas of unbelief, complacency, compromise, or condemnation that you need to identify and confess?

Examine yourself in regard to your relationships with others, including your spouse, children, extended family, friends, business associates, church family, and neighbors. Allow the Holy Spirit to bring to light any areas of unforgiveness, rebellion, neglect, or pride. Write down any names that God brings to mind.

Examine yourself in regard to your spiritual devotion, including time spent in prayer, fasting, reading Scripture, and personal worship. Which areas are lacking in your life? What kinds of changes can you begin to make to address this?

What are some changes that God might be asking you to make in the pursuit of this consecration? Again, this is not about rules, but it is about eliminating the idols and distractions of your life that keep you from a deeper and more intimate relationship with God. It is about addressing areas of weakness in your life that you have been avoiding for far too long.

Write down anything about the areas God is asking you to hand over to Him. Try to come up with some concrete ways you can make changes:

Food (Healthy foods to add, unhealthy foods to avoid)

Health (Exercise, activities, sports)

Media (TV, movies, Internet, etc.)

Time (Cell phones, PDAs, video games, MP3 players, and other distractions)

Other (Anything else in your life that gets in the way of going deeper with God)

I believe it is the heart of God for you to do this with us, and to do so with discipline, accountability, passion, longevity, consistency, and faith. It is my belief that, if you intentionally focus on the task at hand, fairly abiding by whatever boundaries you decide to set, you will find freedom to overcome strongholds, habits, and vices that have controlled you for far too long.

Let's do this for God, for each other, for future generations, and for ourselves. Let's prove we can all start and finish strong!

We Have Overcome

Thanks be to God
Who always causes us to
Triumph in His name
Thanks be to God
Who always causes us to win
Thanks be to God
Thanks be to God

We have overcome
Hallelujah, hallelujah
We have overcome
By the power of Your name
Jesus, You're the one
Hallelujah, hallelujah
The one who made a way
For us to triumph in His name

—by Israel Houghton and Meleasa Houghton
© 2007 Integrity's Praise! Music and Sound of the New Breed (adm
by Integrity's Praise! Music)

CHAPTER ONE

A NEW REALITY

*Delight yourself in the L*ORD
and he will give you
the desires of your heart.
—Psalm 37:4

For a long time, I had a twisted view of that verse. I saw it as a list of things that I wanted and an expectation that God would give them to me—kind of a spiritual fast-food drive-through on the hurried road of life.

I have discovered that the polar opposite is true. I've found that in getting quiet and denying yourself the things that you want, God will then deposit the things He desires into your heart—His purpose, the things He cares about, the deeper things of God.

Then, when you come up for air, you suddenly find yourself thinking, saying, and desiring things you never did before. You begin hearing things you weren't able to tap into with any kind of frequency before. You start believing things and dreaming things and declaring things that weren't there before. This is what I call investing in a new reality.

The Pain of Change

Admit it: Unless you are completely miserable right now, very few of us actually enjoy moving into a season of change, excavation, and sacrifice. Surgery, although sometimes necessary, is rarely something we look forward to. A financial audit, although it can lead to proper planning and stewardship, is not necessarily something we consider fun. So count me as one who actively resists change—especially if it involves messing with my food and entertainment.

In Need of an Upgrade

There are times in life when the plans, desires, hopes, and dreams of our heart begin to run counter to the plans and desires that God has for us. It's not necessarily rebelliousness or ill will on our part. It's just counter to God's plan.

Currently I'm writing this on my new MacBook computer that I received for my birthday. In a perfect world, I can turn this computer on when I feel like it, and then turn it off again when I'm done. Unfortunately, it's not a perfect world, so my beloved Mac began to randomly shut down by itself. This became extremely annoying. For months, I coexisted with the frustration that came with this problem, and I spent hours of fruitless energy trying to figure out the solution on my own. Inevitably, the computer would shut down again, adding to the aggravation and distraction in my life. Eventually I had to go to the computer's maker to get the proper upgrade to fix the problem.

Much like my computer, life has a way of letting you know that it is impossible to proceed peacefully and successfully without the necessary and prescribed upgrade from our Creator in order to function at an optimal level.

Delighting yourself in the Lord requires being still long enough for God to remove the unnecessary parts of our visions, dreams, plans, and desires and to replace them with the upgrades that He has for us. Unfortunately, we often exhaust more energy, resources, and the precious currency of time avoiding this process of elimination and upgrade installation. Then we wonder why we are burning out.

Therefore, I appreciate it when God calls us aside to implant the desires of His heart into ours and to remove yesterday's model of what we once believed to be the ultimate desire and dream for our lives.

I happen to know that Jamil, one of our outstanding vocalists, has a great word picture for this.

A DEEPER LEVEL

Jamil Freeman,
Vocalist
Hometown: Houston, Texas
Get into the River

This water flows toward the eastern region and goes down into the Arabah, where it enters the Sea. When it empties into the Sea, the water there becomes fresh. Swarms of living creatures will live wherever the river flows. There will be large numbers of fish, because this water flows there and makes the salt water fresh; so where the river flows everything will live. (Ezekiel 47:8–9)

Imagine this river is the Holy Spirit, the presence of God, life from God. I personally see it as being gentle and safe, yet deep and expanding as it flows. Imagine this river flowing into the Dead Sea, a body of water too salty to support life. Yet, the river refreshes it so that it *can* support life (our visions, dreams, family, etc.). This is an example of the life-giving nature that flows from our God. God's power can transform us no matter how lifeless or corrupt we may be. Even when we feel messed up and beyond hope, His power can heal us. If we choose to live in this river, we are assured that it will bring forth fruit.

Lord, I pray that You would cause us to pass through waters that are too deep to cross without diving in and swimming. May we be so consumed in this river that we are forever healed and restored, and may this river bring to life whatever lies dormant!

What awesome imagery she has there. Let's follow that line of thinking.

Imagine God as a huge body of water. The only way to fully delight in Him is to dive in headfirst and completely lose yourself in Him.

Something happens when we dive in without concern for the consequences. It is like a surgical procedure in which God implants His desire into our hearts and we emerge saying and believing things we never imagined could happen in our lifetime. We start seeing things differently and walking out what we are newly proclaiming.

From the Head to the Heart

This must go beyond Bible studies and sermons and the acquisition of knowledge. Of course, there is nothing wrong with those things, but I believe that going deeper is accomplished through the heart much more than the mind.

Today, our modern church culture equates going deeper with knowledge. Somehow, if you get more knowledge about something, then you are deeper. If you get out the Hebrew and Greek lexicons, you are deeper. The more degrees and letters you have after your name, the deeper you are spiritually. As good as these things are, Scripture warns us:

We know that we all possess knowledge. Knowledge puffs up, but love builds up. The man who thinks he knows something does not yet know as he ought to know.

(1 Corinthians 8:1–2)

Consider the fact that it was not possible for people to have their own individual Bible until after the printing press was invented in 1450. It was some time later before most people were able to actually afford one. So the entire concept of you, God, and your personal Bible is a relatively new one—only around 500 years old.

Here's my question: How did people go deeper before that?

How did people without Bibles or seminary educations go deeper with God?

We know they did. The first church experienced the presence and power of God through the Holy Spirit and lived in deep fellowship with God. Is it possible that we are too dependent upon our intellect and knowledge?

In America today, most Christian families have several Bibles spread about the home. Many are stuffed in drawers, gathering dust on shelves, or perhaps packed away in boxes with our other spare books. Meanwhile, believers in places where poverty or government intervention prevail—such as China or Africa—often must share a single Bible for an entire church. And yet, missionaries tell us the Spirit of God is moving miraculously in these places. They are certainly going deeper.

At the same time, here in the United States, even with all our education and the resources we possess, many of us still yearn to go deeper with God.

I encourage you to dive into Him today and, of course, dive at the deep end and prepare to be amazed.

Alvin Richardson,
Production Coordinator
Hometown: Baltimore, MD
Out of the Box

I am so excited that God has called us to a deeper level. I'm reminded of a time in the Old Testament when the nation of Israel was called to a deeper level—basically invited to have a closer, more intimate relationship with God. Sounds like a no-brainer, right? But they said, "No thanks." It was too intense for them, too scary. So, instead, God allowed Himself to be figuratively put into a box. They built the Ark of the Covenant to house the Ten Commandments, Moses' rod, and a jar of manna. (See Exodus 16:32–34.) In many ways, however, this box represented the perceived presence of God to the Israelite people. I think God allowed this because He knew that eventually they would get sick of the religion and ritual and would cry out for more.

I can certainly relate to the intensity of closer intimacy with God. We say we want Him near, but do we really want Him around all the time? Do we want Him there when we get cut off in traffic? It can seem a little disconcerting when you think about Him being with you constantly.

Okay, Alvin, let's examine that idea a little more. What would God's continual presence mean for us today?

A DEEPER LEVEL

Alvin Richardson
Blessings Beyond the Box

God has undeniably called us to a deeper level. I believe He wants us to get past the trappings of church culture and lingo and habits. We have the same opportunity that Israel had—will we say "yes"? Or do we secretly prefer for God to stay in the box because it is too scary to have Him so close that our ugliness is exposed. I think we tend to prefer the box. We try to fit Him into a program or a timetable. We repeat the things we say to Him in worship over and over.

Why don't we let God out of the box?

The truth is: we shouldn't be afraid of God cramping our style; we should worry that we will cramp His!

Our faith is boxed in. Our worship is boxed in. Our prayer life is boxed in. Our expectations are boxed in. Let's respond to the call to go to a deeper level and let God out of the box. Let's worship expecting to see the lame walk. Let's sing and play expecting to see limbs grow back. God has already blessed us so much from inside the box—imagine what He will do once we let Him out. During this consecration, find your box and rip it to shreds. There's no telling what God will do.

Beginning a New Habit

If we are going to rip the box to shreds, then that means that this consecration is not going to be something we endure for a period of time and then leave behind. This isn't just a phase we are going through. It isn't a spiritual fad to follow while it's popular. It's a calling. This is going to change us. It is an invitation to go to a new place with God—a place where we will make our dwelling. Wherever God leads us, that will be our new home. What else is going to have to change?

Jamil Freeman
Old Mind-sets

Part of going to a deeper level is changing the way that I think. Going deeper, for me, starts in the mind. Whether I'm fasting, trying to start new habits, or trying to break old addictions, it starts in my mind.

One of my struggles in this journey together is when I revert back to old ways of thinking. Suddenly, my mind tells me that it's okay to do something that I have given up to God. A major part of remaining consistent is overcoming those thoughts. It is refusing to allow my mind to go back to the ways I used to think. It's letting those thoughts drive me to my knees so that I can give all those old feelings, attitudes, and dispositions right back to God.

I can relate to that. I can't tell you how many things I've tried to start, only to quit because I failed to address the way I thought. They say that in order to install a new habit in your life, it takes repetition. But it also takes a mind-set. You have to invest in a new reality where what you once cared for is now not as important. What you once felt was meaningless is now dear to you.

Around day thirty of our fast, for some reason, granola became a food that suddenly tasted phenomenal. Something in me changed. I now valued what I previously considered to be "tree bark" as an incredible, mouth-watering delicacy. Before fasting, I would have laughed if you told me how great a lettuce wrap could taste. But thirty days later, I was different. Suddenly I realized that I had trained my body, will, and emotions in another direction. I'm using food as an example here, but the same thing goes for attitude, mind-sets, spiritual disciplines, and more.

When you wake up in the morning, is the first thing that hits the floor going to be your knees? Will you pick up that Bible early in the morning? You know yourself, and you know your day. If you don't do it first thing, if you don't prioritize it and develop a new habit, the day is going to get away from you as it always does. To start a new habit, you have to invest in the new reality.

Praying as soon as you wake up in the morning may sound extreme right now—much like a discussion about how great lettuce wraps are—but if you start making a habit of it, if you start investing in the new reality, then your priorities will slowly start to change, and a new habit will become established in your life.

Are you committed to investing in the new reality?

What are some new habits that you'd like to see installed into your life?

What changes do you think you will have to make in your day in order for them to become instilled?

What mind-sets are you going to have to set aside in order to invest in the new reality?

CHAPTER TWO

OBSTACLES TO GOING DEEPER

Let us throw off everything that
hinders
and the sin that so easily entangles,
and let us run with perseverance
the race marked out for us.
—Hebrews 12:1

Houston, Texas, where I live, is loaded with incredible restaurants. There is a multitude of ethnic delicacies, Texas barbecue, seafood from the Gulf, and what I believe to be some of the greatest desserts I've ever tasted. And all of it is just a short car ride away.

I'm a big fan of food. So, naturally, the thought of restricting my food intake in any way, shape, or form is not, well, appetizing.

Have you noticed that any time you decide to go deeper spiritually, you will be introduced to obstacles? They may be in the form of a direct spiritual attack to trip you up or they may be the by-product of your own human weaknesses—the physical desires, lusts, and appetites that we'd like to think we control but which, in fact, control us.

There are still other obstacles that are more dangerous and insidious because they are harder to recognize. They don't exist on the surface in the physical; they lie deeper in the heart and are more spiritual in nature.

Seeing It All the Way Through

One of the biggest obstacles for me anytime I start something is seeing it all the way through to the end. As I've led New Breed, we've done a lot of things as a group. We've read books together, we've gone through certain studies, we've even tried to do an exercise regimen together, but, inevitably, there's always a certain percentage of us who don't finish. Nothing dramatic. Nothing super spiritual. Life just gets in the way. They didn't intend to stop. There's no huge reason why they stopped. In fact, if they could spend the energy to find the reason why they couldn't complete the thing, that same energy probably could have carried them through it in the first place.

So, for us, the challenge to finish this consecration came under fire many, many times. To truly finish, to run the entire course and do it right, became the challenge.

Buddy is our keyboard expert. He joins me in the fellowship of those who struggle to finish what they begin.

Arthur "Buddy" Strong,
Keyboards
Hometown: Phoenix, AZ
Encouraged to Complete

I personally have a number of things in my life, spiritually and naturally, that I have started but have yet to complete. I have heard dreams, visions, and goals from many within New Breed—things they want to start or have already started but have not yet completed. There is so much more work to be done. I believe there are songs that have yet to be written that will inspire a new church generation. There are melodies and rhythms that have yet to be played that will drive demons away. There is a standard of lifestyle and character that will rise within us that will set the kingdom on fire. If we will endure and complete the work God has given each one of us, I believe there will be blessings, miracles, signs, and wonders.

> *I have brought you glory on earth by completing the work you gave me to do. And now, Father, glorify me in your presence with the glory I had with you before the world began.* (John 17:4)

OBSTACLES TO GOING DEEPER

I don't know about you, but that fires me up. I need to hear that. I need that kind of encouragement to keep plugging away.

In day-to-day living, what prevents you from going deeper? What challenges you? What tempts you?

We had a forty-day window of time set aside, but it can be even tougher when you don't have a particular goal in mind, when it's just the everyday routine of walking with God. It can be easy, especially for people like me—the creative, non-linear, artist personality—to get all excited about starting something, but get bored or tired halfway through and move on to something else. We artists tend to struggle with regimen.

I've repeated this pattern many times. I made several attempts to do the entire One-Year Bible. I would start strong, but inevitably I'd get behind, and the readings began to stack up. I'd say, "Okay, I am going to catch up tonight." But tonight turned into the next day, and then I was another day behind. Eventually I was able to stick with it and complete it—even if I didn't exactly hit the one-year timeline. After all those failures, to really do it was very rewarding.

Obstacles of the Heart

One of the biggest problems our hearts can hide is the problem of attitude. In worship, that is a huge landmine. We musicians can fall back into relying upon our talent and ability and, as a result, we don't really go as far into worship as we've asked everybody else to go. We remain in the technical area of playing the music. And the better a musician plays or sings, the more people think he or she is worshipping, when in truth he or she is just playing the notes. It's much too easy to do.

We can learn the Christian lingo, all the "God things" to say so that we sound good. No matter what's going on, we tell people that "God is really moving," because this is our worship time and that's what is supposed to be happening. But, in those dry times, we know He's not. We know nothing is going on. Unfortunately, I have been caught in those modes myself.

Thank God for grace, right? Thank God He knows us inside and out; He knows our faulty attitudes and He still loves us anyway.

Here's another great testimony about grace!

Olanrewaju "Lanre" Agbabiaka,
Vocalist
Hometown: Lagos, Nigeria
Sin

Personally, I have struggled with the idea of a life free from sin because it just seems so far-fetched. I knew I was saved, but I still had this human nature to deal with. I simply believed that Jesus was the only one who could truly achieve a sinless state. (I mean, He *is* God, right?)

But, in my study time, God began to shed light on a side of grace that I had missed. I was only familiar with the part of grace that involved my justification and pardon. This was actually my usual escape route from having to deal with the sin stuff in my life—things that, in reality, I wasn't prepared or convinced that I could let go of.

Thank God, I have had a glimpse of the power that lies in grace! Now I am able to graduate from justification to fulfilling God's original plan for my life, which is a life free from the bondage of sin. This is the power that Jesus accessed during His time on earth and *"yet was without sin"* (Hebrews 4:15).

As we journey deeper, I pray we learn to access His power-packed grace in times of need, tests, and trials to help us achieve perfect mastery over sin and be positioned through humility to go even deeper in the revelation of Christ. For as revelation is given, so is grace in all its strength and power.

Obstacle of Busyness

Another big obstacle that requires the grace that Lanre talks about is simply the pace and noise of life. It can so easily knock you off your course. It starts the minute you wake up in the morning. You're ready to rise and shine because this is the day the Lord has made! You are determined to rejoice. Then the alarm goes off, the radio blares, and you stumble out of bed and jam your toe into the leg of your dresser. Instead of praising God, you scream out in pain and frustration. There you go. Welcome to real life.

And life just takes off in a sprint from that moment on. Most of us, maybe not all, but I can certainly speak for myself and the people on my team, tend to live very imbalanced, non-budgeted lives.

Let me explain what I mean by budgeted lives. Bill Hybels, an author and the senior pastor of Willow Creek Community Church in South Barrington, Illinois, really challenged me once when he spoke about the "currency of a day." For me, it was a whole new take on stewardship. I've always been faithful with my financial tithe. I understand that's a part of my life. I also understand that, in order to be a good businessman, I have to budget my money well. So, I've worked hard at that. I realized that managing my money is an area of weakness for me, so I have sought help in that area to ensure that my financial house is in order.

But when Bill Hybels talked about budgeting the "currency of one's day," that really convicted me. Just as with money, we have a limited amount of time to spend each day and each week. What are we going to do with it? Are we going to use it wisely? Are we going to waste it frivolously? I have to wake up in the morning and say, "Okay, how am I going to spend my sixteen or more waking hours?"

I believe that time, life, noise, and the pace of our lives are among the biggest deterrents to going deeper. If you can't manage and maintain your life well, temptation is soon to follow.

Busy, Busy, Busy

Think about it. Our generation is, by far, the busiest of any generation in history. And by busy I mean that we have the ability to constantly be doing a multitude of things at the same time. We are multitasking our way through life. In literally one generation we have gone from horse-drawn carts and outdoor plumbing to a world with automobiles, telephones, radios, airplanes, televisions, computers, the Internet, mobile phones, e-mail, iPods, BlackBerry® handhelds, and whatever comes next.

Past generations would sit at home at night and have conversations or read by the fire. It was easy to get quiet and reflect or read Scripture and pray. Not so today. I can sit in a coffee shop and send e-mails, take phone calls, play video games, and do all kinds of other things—all at the same time! It has become the norm. We can't even dream of not being able to do all of that. How would we function? Some people even do all of that in church!

We tell ourselves that having all of this technology makes our lives simpler, but what it really does is make us much busier. Perhaps it's never been more important to make concerted efforts to incorporate fasting into our spiritual lives. Not just from food, but also from media, from technology, from the noise. I believe it is vitally important to carve out time for silence, solitude, and reflection. If we don't do it, it is not going to present itself to us.

I think we have to seriously ask ourselves if all this technological advancement has really had an impact on the church. I wonder if most of the great books, music, and ideas of the church still come from previous generations that didn't have all the distractions that we have today. They didn't have the Internet and the access to information and connection that we have, but they budgeted their time and were able to become still and have time alone with God in order to receive downloads directly from Him on a consistent basis.

Now don't put me in the crowd that says that all technology is evil. Technology doesn't have a soul. It's not good or bad. It's a tool. And, like any tool, it can be used for good. Thanks to technology, the world has never been smaller. I can stay in touch with our band members in South Africa. I have no doubt that faith pioneers like the apostle Paul would have utilized every bit of technology if it were available to them. But I'm also sure that Paul would have warned us of the dangers of putting these things at the forefront of our lives. He'd warn us that idols aren't only made of stone and wood, sometimes they are made of plastic and electronic circuit boards. Right, Lois?

Lois Du Plessis,
Vocalist
Hometown: Johannesburg,
South Africa
Pulling Down the Gods

One thing I have begun to see in this consecration, without even thinking about it, is what all the various gods are in my life. And it's not just food. I have discovered things that have actually become gods to me—certain TV shows, certain kinds of music that I listen to because it "gets me going." They become gods without us realizing it. We make them our gods.

I suddenly think, *If I don't have this particular cereal in the morning, I can't function.* That sounds ridiculous, but I have made it a god in my life.

We need to use this time to cut out all those little gods that we have put up without even realizing it, because God should be the only god in my life.

Overcoming the Obstacles of Change

Change can be painful, but overcoming that pain can be so good! God is doing something deep in us. Let's remain committed, consistent, and consecrated.

I love Psalm 16. It's a great encouragement when you are fighting to overcome and to install change in your life.

A DEEPER LEVEL

Save me, O God, because I have come to you for refuge.

I said to him, "You are my Lord; I have no other help but yours."

I want the company of the godly men and women in the land; they are the true nobility.

Those choosing other gods shall all be filled with sorrow; I will not offer the sacrifices they do or even speak the names of their gods.

The Lord himself is my inheritance, my prize. He is my food and drink, my highest joy! He guards all that is mine.

He sees that I am given pleasant brooks and meadows as my share! What a wonderful inheritance!

I will bless the Lord who counsels me; he gives me wisdom in the night. He tells me what to do.

I am always thinking of the Lord; and because he is so near, I never need to stumble or to fall.

Heart, body, and soul are filled with joy.

For you will not leave me among the dead; you will not allow your beloved one to rot in the grave.

You have let me experience the joys of life and the exquisite pleasures of your own eternal presence. (PSALM 16 TLB)

If you were honest with yourself, how are you doing so far? How are you doing with some the changes that you want to make in your life?

Don't give up. Even if you have already messed up, don't give up. This is not about perfection or comparing ourselves to others. This is about you going to a deeper level with God. He is calling you forward. No matter what happened yesterday, He calls you forward today. Make the decision to answer the call.

Generally, by about the second week of a journey like this, I begin to second-guess everything about my walk with God. Doubt and fear creep into my head. Because of this, I must make the conscious decision, each day, to follow this journey to the end.

The beauty of this entire process is that God has called us aside to share something intimate and life-changing. The decisions you make today to conduct your life in balance and order will help shape and accelerate the next generation whom God is asking us to lead.

Our children's children are benefiting from the choices we are making today. We've got such a good thing going—don't let go.

What are the biggest obstacles that you face in going deeper with God?

Have you told someone? Have you asked someone to specifically pray for you during this time? Who is it?

CHAPTER THREE

THE DARK PLACES

Fear not,
for I am with you;
Be not dismayed,
for I am your God.
I will strengthen you,
Yes, I will help you,
I will uphold you with
My righteous right hand.
—Isaiah 41:10 (NKJV)

Through this period of fasting and going deeper we can experience dark places within us that we have to deal with. For me, one area that I'm constantly attacked in is my mind and attitude. I start to doubt, and I wonder if all of this is going to make a difference. What's the point? Here I am, pushing people to do something, and I'm sitting here doubting it myself.

I'm a very visual person. I see these things playing out much like a tug-of-war match. Everything in me knows that I'm supposed to confess the Word of the Lord. But there is another side of me that pulls back and asks, "Why am I doing this?" It can be so easy to remain in that area of doubt and fear. Even though I tend to be a very optimistic person, someone who always tries to see the best-case scenario for every situation, still, with the highs come the lows.

If you let them, those lows will just take you down the spiral of self-doubt, fear, and failure to all kinds of dark places. Pretty soon I'm wondering, *Why do I think I can make a difference? Who am I trying to kid? There's this great big world out there with different schools of thought and incredible problems and so many people—What could I possibly do to change things?*

Can anyone relate, or am I alone here?

Michael Clemons,
Drummer
Hometown:
Virginia Beach, VA
Fear!

I'm with Israel in this! By day twelve of our consecration, all I could hear in my head was, *I can't do this!* I opened the Bible and quickly saw the word *fear*. I looked it up. "Fright, terror, alarm, panic, trepidation, dread, anxiety…" These were all things I was feeling before seeing them spelled out in black and white.

After 9/11, many of us walked around in fear of not wanting to get on an airplane. Being a father and husband, I fear not being able to provide for my family. These are typical human fears.

But there are also spiritual fears. The enemy wants me to be defeated before I even try to complete my God-given assignment. In my process of consecration, the evil one wanted to play upon the fear he *thought* I had. You see, the devil can put it in our minds that we can't do something. But if we speak, believe, and live God's Word, how can faith and fear live within the same house? Check out what the Bible says about overcoming fear: Psalm 112:7–8; Isaiah 41:10; and 2 Timothy 1:7.

There's a great concept: how can faith and fear live in the same house? That is so true. Because, somewhere deep within, I have faith—a belief—that I was put on this earth, in this generation, to help change the world. Whatever the world looks like, whatever my part of the world is, I am here to help make a deep impact on it. I'm going to do that. In light of that revelation, fear takes flight, things shift, and my attitude changes.

We generally need some help to chase fear from our hearts. We need to get quiet with God. We need to engage in a fast, a reprioritizing of our lives to cut out the distractions. Only then can we begin to deal with the doubt and the fear and the crises of confidence, because we can stay so busy in our lives that we never fully deal with them. We bury them under appointments and responsibilities and commitments and we are never able to become still and address the dark places.

Have you ever had company coming over and the house is a mess? What do you do? You shove everything in a closet, right? Your guests arrive and think your house is so neat and that you are so tidy. But you know the truth. Eventually someone ventures toward the closet and asks, "So what's in this room?" And you lunge at them, shouting, "No!"

It's like that in our dark inner places, isn't it? We keep shoving all that doubt and fear and guilt to the background, stashing them in closets, and we just go on with all of our busyness. But when you quiet down, limit the distractions, and invite God in, eventually He's going to wander over toward that closet and ask, "So what's in there?"

"No!"

Now you are forced—like Jacob—to wrestle with a God who wants to do some housecleaning. (See Genesis 32:24-30.) Hopefully, we can get to the place where we can trust God in the midst of the struggle. We can realize that He is not out to get us. We can actually go through the struggle with Him—and survive.

From: **Mattie Blackburn**,
Vocalist
Hometown: Dallas, TX
No Fear!

Recently, God has been dealing with me about fear. I'm not talking about stage fright or a fear of large crowds; I'm talking about the kind of fear that grips you hard enough to derail your life course. Throughout this consecration, there will be several areas of our lives that need to be realigned. Beyond just starting some habits or shedding a few pounds, mostly I want God to take fear from my heart.

When I was a young girl growing up in a strict home, we didn't speak much about the confidence that we could have in God. We did, however, speak a whole lot about the fear we should have of God. It was to the point that I fully expected God to come down here and whack me over the head for not being perfect enough.

Only recently have I understood that my being fulfilled is more important to God than my chastisement. God desires that, above all else, His will for your life be made complete. What does that mean for each one of us? What are you fearful of? Who are you fearful of? Do you sometimes self-destruct right before a breakthrough of purpose?

The thing about fear is this: there's nothing to be gained by it. It's kind of like sugar in your diet—it has taste, but no nutritional value. So what's the point in having it? If it doesn't add value to your life, throw it out!

There's a sermon right there. There's nothing to be gained by fear. And yet, some of us hold on to fear tightly and refuse to follow Mattie's advice: throw it out!

Ego

Another dark place, especially for those of us who serve God very publicly—on a huge stage with big spotlights—is our ego. For us musicians, we've worked hard at our craft, rehearsed, and spent years practicing our instruments. Then, after we serve God on a Sunday, people come up, pat us on the back, and say, "Good job!" And it's not just the music team. They do that to other artists such as dancers and actors, depending on your church. They certainly do it to preachers.

They don't do that to those who serve in certain other ministries. When was the last time anyone praised the person in the nursery?

"Great job changing that diaper during the first service!"

When was the last time someone complimented the parking lot attendant?

"That was amazing when you stood out there in the rain for an hour and directed traffic!"

Or how about the youth worker?

"What an awesome job you did of investing in those junior high boys for two hours on a Thursday night! Way to go!"

Certainly there's nothing wrong with giving or receiving a little encouragement, but it's a very small leap to adoration—where we are accepting the praise, instead of giving it up.

For that reason, we are constantly reminding ourselves that we are to be lenses and not mirrors. That means we are to be looked through and not necessarily looked at.

At the same time, one of the things I've been encouraging New Breed to see in recent months is that we should err on the side of confidence in believing that we are playing a part in making history right now. Therefore, we should take the gifts and ministry that God has given us very seriously. We need to walk humbly and graciously in the knowledge that others are watching us. We should not downplay the influence we have on others and begin to live our lives loosely.

Jerry Harris,
Music Director/Keyboards
Hometown:
Portland, OR

Does God Need Our Gifts?

I was nosing around in my wife's Bible when I saw a paragraph talking about how often we try to bargain with God. We think that with good deeds and our measly sacrifices—things like singing and playing, being on time, giving someone a ride home, giving someone in need a little spare change—we can try to manipulate God into putting His stamp of approval on our plans. Even typing that appalls me, but we do it.

Psalm 50:9–12 says, *"I have no need of a bull from your stall or of goats from your pens, for every animal of the forest is mine, and the cattle on a thousand hills. I know every bird in the mountains, and the creatures of the field are mine. If I were hungry I would not tell you, for the world is mine, and all that is in it."*

Remember, a gift is something given voluntarily, without compensation. We can't buy our way into God's good graces. We aren't that gifted! We can't earn our way through sacrifice, especially when what we would call "sacrifice," God would call the norm.

God said, *"The world is mine, and all that is in it."*

What a great reminder, Jerry. How easily we can overestimate the value of our gifts. How easily we can start to take credit for them and see ourselves as special—as living in rarified air.

Throughout the years, I have had the chance to meet some of my heroes, people that I have really looked up to. But sometimes, meeting them was a letdown. It seemed as if they smelled their own victory. They were so cocooned within their own success that they couldn't be bothered with somebody insignificant like me—someone who could do nothing for them.

That has taught me to be proactive in dealing with how our team treats people, and what to say when somebody is paying us a compliment. When somebody is thanking us or expressing his or her appreciation for our music, we should not brush that off. We need to give God all the glory, of course, but we need to look that person in the eyes and thank them. Often, God uses us to touch people's lives through music and worship, and it is such a privilege to know that we had a part in a moment like that.

The second you start believing that you are the reason forty people were saved tonight, you're in trouble. I've seen so many people get caught up in the adoration and the attention that they started to believe their own press and appreciate their own anointing.

Empowerment Begins

My worship career began when I was just nineteen years old. Growing up, I was always that kid who jumped on the drums after the service and annoyed everybody. Eventually, they let me play in the worship bands. Then, one Wednesday afternoon, I got a call from the pastor, saying, "Hey, would you consider being our worship leader?"

I said something spiritual, like, "Well, Pastor, I don't know. I'll pray about it." Of course, everything in me was saying, "Absolutely not!"

But the pastor replied, "Okay, I'll tell you what. Start praying really hard and really fast, because you start tonight!"

So there I am, on stage every week singing the same three Ron Kenoly songs. The pastor tried to encourage me by telling me, "You're anointed. I just know you're anointed." Of course that didn't sit well, because he was the same guy sitting with his wife just a few feet in front of me during worship. I could hear them talking. She would say, "Baby, this is awful." He'd say, "I know. This is powerfully awful."

I was up there singing, and I wanted to shout, "I can hear you!"

For six weeks straight, every Sunday night after the service, I would go to that pastor and say, "Hey, Pastor, praise God. I quit. I just quit. There's got to be someone else."

Every week he'd answer back, "Okay, that's all right. I'll see you tomorrow." And every week, I'd get the call: "You're leading worship this week."

Sister Sandpaper

You know how every choir has that one person—I'll call her Sister Sandpaper. She's self-elected, and it is her civic choir duty to tell you what isn't working. Every Sunday night, just before I'd quit again, Sister Sandpaper would come to me and say, "Well, that didn't work." "Pastor doesn't like that song." "It's too high." "That one soprano yelling on the mic? That isn't working." "Your soprano's dress is too short." "We heard that your drummer smokes."

It's always something with Sister Sandpaper.

One Sunday, I have to admit—it was bad. I think the drummer may have thrown his sticks at me at some point during the service. It just wasn't happening. Afterward, I saw Sister Sandpaper coming my way. Sister said, "You know, I figured it out. Do you know what your problem is?"

Now understand, I was this insecure, nineteen-year-old kid. I was the only black guy in the place. I felt totally beat up and was planning to quit once again. It took everything in me not yell back at her, "Yes, ma'am, I do. You! You are my problem! Thank you for asking! If you would just leave the church, we'd be just fine!"

But I didn't. Somehow, my inner monologue didn't burst out. What did come out was a slightly sarcastic reply, "No, why don't you tell me?"

Sister didn't bat an eye and said, "You're working out your stuff on our time."

Ouch!

You see, God sometimes sends a Sister Sandpaper into your life to tell you the things you do not want to hear—but that you absolutely need to hear. The purpose of sandpaper is to smooth out the rough edges. The problem is, you don't get smooth without some friction.

I remember thinking, "Man! Am I bleeding? She just cut me!"

But I had a realization that completely changed me in that moment. The stuff that Sister referred to was worship. In that moment, I realized that the only time I worshipped was when I was on that stage.

When do you worship?

Be honest now. Is the only time you ever worship during those fifteen minutes at the beginning of the service?

Working It Out in the Kitchen

At that time, I shared a little house with Ricardo, a guitarist in my band. I went home and we pushed this little black upright piano into the kitchen because it had a lot of tile that created a natural reverb and great acoustics. I opened up my Bible to random psalms, and I began to play and sing the things I was reading. I played things I had never rehearsed. I played things I had never played before or since. And the more time I spent in that kitchen, the easier it flowed.

No one will ever hear the things I played there. Those songs remain embedded in the walls of that kitchen. But something started happening. I started to hear God sing back. I started seeing things and hearing things. God was saying things like, "If you will just stay with Me like this, I will take you to the ends of the earth—if I can trust you."

Isn't it funny how much time we spend telling Him, "God, I'm trying to figure out if I can trust You." What is that? He's God. Of course we can trust Him to do what's best for us.

You need to understand that God is trying to get you to a place where He knows that He can trust you.

This whole kitchen experience became kind of like a drug. I couldn't wait to get home, not to watch some TV show, but to get back in the kitchen! I yearned to sit at that piano and say, "God, what else are we going to talk about? What else do You want to say to me? How else can I praise You? What else can I get out of this word?"

Here's the most amazing thing: the better things got in the kitchen, the better things got publicly. Unfortunately, the better things got publicly, the less time I spent in the kitchen.

Now, the same people who were saying, "I don't know about this boy," were now the ones saying, "I always knew you were anointed." Things were changing and moving. Now I had man's approval! My pastor started to talk me up and brag about me to others. Suddenly I was traveling and people were taking notice.

But back in the kitchen, the piano was beginning to gather dust, a pile of bills, and maybe an old sandwich. Because now it was working. I loved the Lord. I was faithful. People were being ministered to and healed and blessed. It was awesome.

I remember thinking, *Lord, thank You for that season in the kitchen, but I've got this now. I've got some songs and tapes. I'm good.*

Watch out when your heroes begin to tell you, "Man, you're all right. You're anointed. You keep that up."

Your First Love

Inevitably, we all go through a season, maybe some of you are in that season right now, where no matter where you go or what you hear—a song, a sermon, a testimony, a conversation—you keep hearing the same thing over and over. God just hammers away at you on a daily basis on the same message.

I hadn't been in the kitchen for quite a while. But for a six- or seven-week period, no matter where I went, someone would begin to talk about a particular passage. It's the one in Revelation where Jesus addressed the church at Ephesus:

> *I know your works, your labor, your patience, and that you cannot bear those who are evil. And you have tested those who say they are apostles and are not, and have found them liars; and you have persevered and have patience, and have labored for My name's sake and have not become weary.*
> (Revelation 2:2–3 NKJV)

Right about here I was ready to pat myself on the back. I thought, You're right, Lord. I've been faithful. I've persevered. I've been serving You. Then comes what is for me the biggest *"nevertheless"* in Scripture:

> **Nevertheless** *I have this against you, that you have left your first love.* (Revelation 2:4 NKJV)

At first, I would hear it and think, *Praise the Lord! Whoever that's for, Lord, I pray You would touch them.*

A couple of days later, I'd talk to my dad, and he'd tell me about a song he heard that talked about returning to your first love.

The next week, someone at church would give a testimony where they referenced Revelation 2:4.

But still I thought, *Wow, God really wants to speak to somebody.*

After three or four times, I begin to suspect it was for my good friend, Aaron. I prayed for him and laid hands on him, that he might receive this word.

Eventually, I was leading worship for a group of pastors and worship leaders when something happened. People were kneeling down front and crying. When the lead pastor got up to speak, he changed what he was going to do and suggested that we just stay in this place of worship.

I don't know who came up with the concept (it was probably Lucifer), but there can be times that we think that what goes on in worship is a credit to us. This was one of those moments. I turned to my friend Aaron:

"This is awesome, man. He can't even preach!"

He replied, "Man, you're sweet in the anointing."

"No, you're the one."

"No, you da man."

"No, you da man!"

"No, we da men!"

As we were there slapping each other on the back, this leader then said, "Now, before I put this mic down, I just feel the need to tell you to go back to your first love."

At that moment, I just stopped where I was, closed my eyes, and what I saw was this nineteen-year-old punk pushing his piano into his kitchen.

I heard the Lord say, "You know, Israel, I enjoyed My time better with you when you didn't know anything. I enjoyed My time with you when you were totally relying on Me to do it. Come back."

I fell on my face. A long time later, when I came out of it, it was like I was born again—again. And my prayer was, "Lord, help me to unlearn some stuff."

I had turned into someone who thought, *Look what the Lord has done, but, you know, I had something to do with it!* It wasn't something that came out of my mouth, it wasn't something I dwelled on, but it was definitely germinating in my heart. And it was evident in my fruit.

Empowerment versus Entitlement

When that nineteen-year-old kid was called to lead worship, that was empowerment. I was completely unqualified, but God used somebody in my life to say, "I believe in you. Let's try that again."

"But, Pastor, I made a mess of the service. It was horrible."

"I know. It was awful. But let's try it again."

Empowerment is being elevated or promoted by others who sense any hint of power or qualification in your life.

Back in the day, my leg would start to twitch nervously before I went on to lead worship. I would be thinking, *O God, if You don't show up....help us, Lord!*

But somewhere empowerment became entitlement.

That's when you start thinking that you belong. You start thinking, *I deserve this.* And suddenly all of that humility and the privilege and the honor of being used by God subtly becomes:

"What would you all do without me?"

"If I left here, this place just wouldn't know what to do."

"They are so lucky to have me here."

It is a fine line. Mine was a spirit that needed to be broken. It's a spirit today that needs to be broken in individuals; it's a spirit that has to be broken in us as a body.

Leaving the Praise at His Feet

Jesus said that, when you do a good thing, "*do not announce it with trumpets, as the hypocrites do in the synagogues and on the streets, to be honored by men. I tell you the truth, they have received their reward in full*" (Matthew 6:2).

I don't want that.

When kids come up and thank us and say they love our music and listen to it all the time, I want to use that moment for God. I want to encourage them more than they have encouraged me. I want to tell them about all the great things that they are going to do for God. And the thing is, to do all that only takes a few seconds. But it is a few seconds that God might use to shape the direction of that person's life. So, instead of feeding our own ego, we are really trying to seize those moments and make each one count.

The truth is, we work hard at our craft. We spend countless hours rehearsing. When I learned guitar, I spent six hours a day—every day—practicing and trying to develop the skill. After all those years of hard work and diligent effort, when somebody says, "Hey man, you're great," you can't help but appreciate that. And when you are fortunate enough to be recognized by your peers and your industry with a Dove Award or a Grammy, you can't help but feel the satisfaction that all that hard work paid off.

But at the end of the day, I have to take that Grammy and all the accolades and put them at the feet of Jesus because if I ever start looking at what I have done—it's over.

I know what I deserve. And I certainly didn't deserve promotion. I certainly didn't deserve to be any kind of praise and worship leader that anybody knows. I don't deserve to win awards for worshipping Jesus!

I've made mistakes. I've done some dumb stuff, said some dumb stuff, and acted out some dumb things. And I can tell you that the spirit of entitlement nearly took me down.

More than We Deserve

I know what I deserve. I deserve hell. We all deserve hell. But God said, "I'll tell you what I'm going to do..."

When I was sixteen, I got caught sneaking out of the house. My mother said, "Either you tell your father or I will." So I went to my dad expecting to be punished. I had no choice but to tell it like it was.

"Uh, Dad? Look, I got caught sneaking out of the house. Sorry. So, do whatever you have to do."

My dad looked at me and said, "What do you think I ought to do?"

I said, "Dad, look, I have a track meet on Friday. Do whatever you want but please let me go to the track meet." Then I believe I started to cry and grovel.

My dad was just smiling at me. "I'll tell you what I'm going to do. I'm going to give you a later curfew."

"What's that, Dad? I beg your pardon?"

"Yeah, you're getting older, you're driving, I'm going to let you come home at eleven instead of ten."

I didn't know how to respond. I almost would have felt better if he would have yelled at me and punished me. But he didn't do that.

Isn't that just like God?

The problem is, most of us didn't grow up understanding that we are a friend of God. Most of us grew up being afraid of God, believing that at any moment He was going to come down on us with the hammer of justice.

Instead, God says, "I'll tell you what I'm going to do. I'm

going to make you a royal priesthood. I'm going to make you part of a holy nation. I'm going to set you apart as a chosen people, a chosen generation." (See 1 Peter 2:9.)

Why would He do that? Does He know who He just invested that kind of trust into? I'm a mess! But God says, "Let's work it out."

Thank God that we belong to Him. Thank God that He belongs to us. But the second that we start thinking, *I belong. I'm here because I did it right.*

Danger.

Here's my challenge to you. Take inventory right now. You've started on a journey. For some of you, the gradual advance of sin is undetectable until it eventually bumps you off course. Suddenly you are no longer empowered by others; now it's all about the entitlement you expect from others. It becomes twisted. Suddenly the expectation and the electricity, that good nervousness and leg twitching that goes with coming into God's presence, gives way to something else and you become familiar with the presence and the glory. Like Uzzah, you reach up and casually touch the ark any time you want. (See 1 Chronicles 13:9–10.)

You've lost the place of your first love.

It's not necessarily a rebellion where you declare, "I'm not going there anymore!" It's a gradual thing. It's fewer visits to the kitchen, less time in His presence. So let's reflect and get honest.

In what ways does fear affect you?

Spend some time in Scripture and find a verse that refutes that. Ask someone for help if you can't find one. When you find it, memorize it.

In what areas do you struggle with ego or pride? Is it in the area of knowledge? Or talent? Or strength? How does it affect your faith? How do you handle it if someone compliments you?

In what ways have you perhaps secretly felt entitled? Have you ever felt yourself thinking, *They're pretty lucky to have me here*? Where does that come from?

Some of us haven't heard God's voice in a very long time. There are songwriters out there who can't remember the last time they wrote a song. There is new inspiration and creativity available. God wants to tell you, "Here's what I see. Let's do this together."

If you will just return to your first love.

I Will Search for You

How precious, how lovely
Are Your thoughts, O Lord, toward me
How truly amazing
Is the grace that You have shown
O Majesty, I live to see Your face

I will search for You
And I will find You
I will find You with all my heart
I will lift my hands to You and worship
And I will worship with all my heart

How gracious, relentless
Is the Father's love toward us
Breathtaking, the beauty
And the radiance of You
O Majesty, I live to see Your face
And be transformed into Your image

Oh, I will worship You with all my heart

—by Israel Houghton and Meleasa Houghton

CHAPTER FOUR

CHARACTER VERSUS ANOINTING

Listen, O coastlands, to Me, and
*   take heed, you peoples from*
*   afar!*
The LORD has called Me from the
*   womb;*
From the matrix of My mother He
*   has made mention of My name.*
And He has made My mouth like a
*   sharp sword;*
In the shadow of His hand He has
*   hidden Me,*
And made Me a polished shaft;
*   In His quiver He has hidden Me.*
*   —Isaiah 49:1–2 (NKJV)*

ave you ever driven through a town that has a large industrial factory that emits a pungent odor? You get out of your car and the first thing you do is crinkle your nose and ask, "How do people live here?"

What is the inevitable answer?

"You just get used to it." The people who live there are accustomed to it. It's become the norm.

That was the spiritual state of Israel in the middle of 2 Chronicles. They had endured a virtual parade of fallen, sinful men who served as their king. One chapter after another seems to begin with, "And so and so became king and he did evil in the sight of the Lord, just like his father did. And he had a son, and he did evil, too. And so and so was born, and he was a mess, too."

On and on the story goes, generation after generation. I remember reading it on an airplane once and really starting to hunger for someone good to come along. Then, finally, along comes twenty-five-year-old Hezekiah. He becomes king, and Scripture says that *he did what was right in the sight of the Lord* (2 Chronicles 29:2 NJKV). When I read that, I think I let out a cheer right there in the plane and startled the lady next to me. I leaned over and told her, "Yeah, Hezekiah. He's one of the good ones."

By the time he became king, the song of the Lord had not been sung in many generations. He came to the temple and, in effect, said, "Something stinks!" The first thing he had to do was repair the very doors to the temple. (See 2 Chronicles 29:3.) When they got inside, he even had to have the priests carry rubbish out of the Holy Place! (See verse 5.)

It reminds me of the fable of the frog in the boiling pot. The story says that if you put a frog in boiling water he will hop right out. But if you put him in cold water and slowly raise the temperature, he will boil to death as the water gradually gets warmer and warmer. Because of the gradual progression of change, the frog never becomes alarmed until it is too late.

I've seen some "frogs" dying within Christian worship ministries, and I'm sure the same holds true in other areas of the church. I've seen people in high-level ministries who have the talent, the gifting, even the anointing, but have zero lifestyle to back it up.

I've been there. After I came out of that kitchen, I knew that I had an anointing for this time and this generation. I knew how to play and sing. I learned all the right worship phrases to shout out. But I had no private life of devotion to back up the anointing.

There are some talented singers in the secular music industry who can sing a gospel song that will have you wiping tears from your eyes. They have an anointing, something more than merely talent. Somehow, God reaches out and touches your soul when they sing.

You see, the anointing is irrevocable—it is yours for life. The anointing is the gift God gives you. Character is the gift you give back in return.

As Buddy knows, as exciting as it is to be up on stage in front of a crowd, there is a very sober and humbling side as well.

A DEEPER LEVEL

Buddy Strong
God's Completion

Many people see and hear us on TV, buy our CDs, or experience us in a live concert, and have the perception of us being complete in our career, complete in our ministry, or just complete all around. I have actually heard people say, "If I can just get to where you are, I will be good."

Yikes.

I pray that, through this consecration, there will be a standard in our lifestyle and in our character that will rise within us to set the kingdom on fire. But God will have to do the work in us.

Some of us have made a quick start in our ministry and career, but there will come a time when we will have to slow down, wait, and have patience. We will be able to move only when God says move. No matter how strong we are spiritually and naturally, there will come a time when we won't be able to overpower a problem or situation like usual. May God complete the hard work that He has begun in us.

There's a man who realizes that with great gifting comes great responsibility. Unfortunately, most people only focus on the gifting and not the responsibility. So how can we develop a character that backs up our anointing?

A Chosen Arrow

Let's look again at the verse from Isaiah at the beginning of this chapter:

> *Listen, O coastlands, to Me, and take heed, you peoples from afar! The LORD has called Me from the womb; from the matrix of My mother He has made mention of My name. And He has made My mouth like a sharp sword; in the shadow of His hand He has hidden Me, and made Me a polished shaft; in His quiver He has hidden Me.* (Isaiah 49:1–2 NKJV)

Or, in another version it substitutes *"polished shaft"* with *"He has also made Me a select arrow"* (verse 2 NASB).

In Isaiah's day, it took a lot more effort to make an arrow. Today we go to a sporting goods store and pick out a machine-lathed, graphite, aerodynamically engineered arrow. In Isaiah's day, it was hard work.

The archer would go into the woods and take a branch from an acacia tree, a hard wood with a lot of knots in it. They didn't have saws or sandpaper, so he would start cutting away at the knots in the wood with stones. He would get it to a place where he could peg it down between two rocks—kind of like putting it in a vise. Then he would boil it to harden it even further. Finally, he would just leave it in the sun to bake.

It was vitally important to get that shaft smooth and straight so that the arrow would fly true and hit the target at which it was aimed. An arrow with a crooked shaft, no matter how sharp the head, was worthless to the archer.

Of course, you are the arrow in this metaphor. Unfortunately, some churches place all their focus upon the arrowhead. I have approached pastors I served with in ministry and said, "Listen, I'm not doing very well here. There are some things in my heart that I need some help with. I'm struggling with my attitude." I literally had one pastor say to me, "Just shut up and sing."

Why? Because the arrowhead was sharp. The music was good. Attendance was up. Tithing was up. Shut up and sing; your arrowhead is sharp.

That may be, but the shaft was crooked. I had no character. I had not been fathered. I was crying out, "Mess with me, get in my face, help me."

Just shut up and sing.

Far too often it becomes, "Can she sing? Does she look good? Put her up there." "Can he play? Do people like him? Put him up there." And it goes beyond just music. There are deacons and elders and Sunday school teachers in the same boat. "Does she have the experience we need? Does she tithe? Put her on the board." "Does he show up for junior high ministry? Do the kids like him? Put him up there."

I spent a season just getting sanded. Was it painful? Absolutely. I got some phone calls from other churches saying, "Hey, you want to come over here? We don't have all that heavy-handed stuff. We don't worry about all of that; we just want you to sing all those songs that people like."

Part of the problem is fathers who don't want to father. But the other part of it is sons and daughters who say, "I want to be fathered, but I don't want to be bothered."

Here's the brutal truth: the life expectancy of most worship leaders in any one place is just three years. And I think that's a bit generous. Too many worship leaders, after three years, say, "I've got to find a new thing."

Too many churchgoers are really church shoppers. They are looking for the church that will move their emotions but stay out of their business. The minute a pastor tries to prod or open a few closet doors, they are off to find another church.

Our great Arrow Maker wants to apply sand to the rough areas of our lives. The tragedy is that too many Christians have a nomadic spirit that says, "If you get too close, if you challenge my life, I'm going to bolt because this church down this street is going to let me tithe and serve, and they're going to leave me alone." In doing so, these believers have established a detour around the important process of sanctification—being made holy through the sanding of prayer, confession, and repentance.

Jennifer Houghton,
Operations Manager
Hometown: Santa Fe, NM
Our Example

When I was younger, we would sing a chorus, "I Want to Be More Like You, Jesus." I would think, *How am I ever going to be like Him? Jesus is holy and I am so, well, unholy!* In this consecration I have found myself looking back over my life and especially at all the things I wish I would have done a bit differently or better, which got me thinking that it's never too late to start working on being more like Jesus. In order to begin **NOW** on a path of holiness, even at this stage of my life, I would have to follow the best example of a life of integrity—Jesus.

He is the only one I know of who was completely committed to doing God's will in His life. By dying on the cross, He made a way for us to *"come boldly before the throne"* (Hebrews 4:16). Our sins no long longer separate us from God. He has made a way for us to come to Him in repentance and to worship Him for who He is. When our deepest longing is to recognize the holiness of God, then we can seek to be holy as He is holy. I believe it is possible for us to truly know the heart of God, and the things that concern and move His heart. It is when we begin to know His heart that we can lead by example.

Straighten the Shaft

When God reaches back into His quiver and pulls out an arrow, I want to be a *"select arrow."* Not just because my arrowhead is sharp. Most of us spend far more time honing the talent and the gifting than we do making sure the shaft is straight. Why? Because there doesn't seem to be a very lucrative market for character. On the other hand, there's always a market for good singing and good writing. "We love those songs, man." Your gift is sharp.

If you only work on the arrowhead, when you are released from the bow, you're going to hit something. But if that shaft is not straight, you're going to do damage. And you're not going to do damage to the kingdom of darkness; you're going to do damage to the kingdom of God.

Let's look at it from the point of view of a church vocalist. We see the steps of elevation. "I'm going to join the choir, but eventually I'm going to get a mic. I'm going to sing in the choir, but I'm going to sing loud and get right next to that hanging mic. I might have to step on some folks to get there, but I'm going to get that mic."

Think about why you wanted to get involved in church music to begin with. You were in church and you saw those "icons" on stage with their mics—the frontline singers. It's the *us* and *them* mentality. They're in the choir; I'm on the front line.

Then you get that mic. Now, the pastor will know that I'm as talented as anybody here. I'm as anointed as anybody here.

We see these as steps to get somewhere.

But when your emphasis is on character instead of talent—the shaft instead of the arrowhead—you can stand in the back of the choir, far from the mic; you can wear those colors that you don't like wearing; and you can say, "Lord, keep sanding. Take a look. Is it straight? Close? Then just deal with this knot right here."

The gift that God gave you is your gift for life. Character is the gift you have to give back. Here's the challenge: everybody is looking for a shortcut to greatness, except for the people of God. People of the kingdom need to say, "Lord, what does it take to establish longevity in my bloodline, in my legacy, in my children? Let me do the work!"

Stacey Joseph,
Vocalist
Hometown:
Baton Rouge, LA
On the Inside

"Behold, You desire truth in the inward parts, and in the hidden part You will make me to know wisdom" (Psalm 51:6 NKJV). Here David is lamenting over the sin he committed with Bathsheba after being confronted by the prophet Nathan. Being convinced and convicted of his sin, he pours out his soul to God in prayer for mercy and grace. This Scripture begins with what God desires—truth in the inward parts. God's work in me is to "make me to know wisdom." He will give me inside information, His way of doing things, so that my life may fulfill His desire.

David's sin was colored by adultery and premeditated murder. Our sin may be colored by an unruly tongue, pride, selfishness, deceit, _____ (you fill in the blank). But God's desire is still the same—truth from the inside out. If we allow Him to go deep within us, to enlighten our minds, and to create a new heart, He then gains our will.

CHARACTER VERSUS ANOINTING

Many of us came into the kingdom of God as a part of a cursed bloodline—family dysfunctions such as divorce, infidelity, abuse, addiction, or other discouraging realities. It stops with us. And it doesn't just stop with us; something new starts with us.

We can just rely on our anointing—the arrowhead—and sing our way around all the sanding and straightening that needs to be done. Or, we can say, "For the sake of my children, I'm going to undergo the sanding, the surgical procedure that needs to be done in order to become a select arrow—a polished shaft. I want to be used like that."

Remove the Rubbish

Unfortunately, I have walked into some churches and choirs where I wanted to say, "Oh, man, what is that smell? What is the spirit of that place? How can they stay here?"

And people will tell you, "Oh, they just got used to it."

Stop living beneath the privilege of a child of God. What can you do to freshen the air? What can you do to become the kind of leader, the kind of servant, the kind of worshipper who is a catalyst for change? How can you become one who needs no prompting or demanding, but just says, "Lord, I get to be in Your presence today. It's so great to be here."

When you get there you will be able to say this:

The thing of which I am a part...
Is greater than the part I play.

Let's say it again:

**The thing of which I am a part...
Is greater than the part I play.**

When you start to realize that, you will realize you are empowered to be here, but you aren't entitled to be here. It's a privilege to be here; it's not an obligation to be here. Then, stuff will start happening.

What would happen with that kind of expectation?

Thank you for being anointed and for being gifted. Thank you, vocalists and instrumentalists and deacons and elders and ushers and Sunday school teachers, for serving God's people the way you have. But this is a moment of inventory for you. This is one of those God-ordained moments.

How is your arrow? And I am *not* talking about the arrowhead.

Can you say, "My character matches my anointing?"

To be blatantly honest, to take some of the pressure off—mine does not. Not yet. But I've submitted to the process. I've said, "Lord, keep sanding, keep teaching me, harass me." I'm doing this because I want longevity. I don't want to merely travel to the back of the auditorium; I want to go to the ends of the earth.

It's easy to find shortcuts to greatness.

This is a moment where God says, "Can I trust you to stay pegged down? Can I sand down the rough edges? Can you stick it out where you are one more year? Let Me show you what I can do. It's easy to run; don't run."

Do you have a mentor? Do you have someone who knows you and can tell you the hard truth? Who is it?

If not, who might that person be? You might need to go to them and give them permission to speak into your life.

Has God done some sanding in your life? Briefly describe that and thank Him.

If not, how have you avoided the hard work that goes with becoming a _"select arrow"_?

CHAPTER FIVE

A DEEPER WORSHIP

Let the heavens rejoice,
Let the earth be glad;
Let the sea resound, and all that
*   is in it;*
Let the fields be jubilant,
And everything in them.
Then all the trees of the forest will
*   sing for joy;*
*They will sing before the L*ORD*.*
                              —Psalm 96:11–13

Let's get one thing straight. We were made to worship. Because it is a basic part of who we are, we all worship. It's as essential to us as breathing air, drinking water, and eating food. It is something we must do because we were made to do it.

That's right, everybody worships. Just turn on your TV and see how fixated we become on people like Paris Hilton, Brad Pitt, or the late Anna Nicole Smith. Go to the magazine rack at the grocery store checkout line and see how we adore knowing every little detail about those we worship. We flock to rock concerts to adore our heroes. We follow movie stars to see anything they do in the theaters. Grown men spend money to play fantasy baseball and football, obsessing over the statistics of twenty-year-old boys! There is something within each one of us that drives us to worship something, anything. It may not be God, but we will worship something!

Worship in the Church

I wish I could say that we in the church have this worship thing down. Unfortunately, we don't. And this is especially true in the Christian music industry where in the last few years worship music has exploded and suddenly become (gulp!) profitable.

Think of the titles we have given to the legends of the secular music industry: Michael Jackson, "the King of Pop"; Elvis Presley, "the King of Rock 'n' Roll"; and Aretha Franklin, "the Queen of Soul." Unfortunately, this has also happened in the Christian music industry where similar titles are given to artists.

Obviously this is a dangerous thing. Such "Luciferian oxymorons" remind us that the original fall was not Adam, but heaven's worship leader.

A reporter once asked me, "If so-and-so is the King and if so-and-so is the Queen, then what are you?"

My first inclination was to blurt out something dismissive like, "I'm a just a friend of God." But my mind went in a different direction.

I said, "I'm the court jester."

The interviewer was caught a little off guard.

She wondered, "What's a court jester?"

I tried to explain that, with all these images of royal and exalted positions, the court jester was the guy who wore the funny hat, played an instrument, and whose sole intent was to entertain the king and make him laugh. If the king was pleased with his performance, he got to live another day. If the king didn't laugh, if he frustrated the king, if he irritated the king, it was "off with his head!" A lot of court jesters gave their lives because they were having a bad day.

Now, that may be a little morbid, and certainly our God is full of more grace and love than some medieval king, but I like the picture of coming into the presence of the Lord and playing for Him alone. It's so easy to lose track of that, especially for a musician who is entertainment-minded. It is a sad commentary that there are probably several headless worship leaders and artists out there who may not realize that they have lost their head due to the fact that the King is not pleased.

When I play at a church, I can easily lapse into thinking, I really hope the pastor digs it, or I hope the crowd is jumping up and down and into it. The truth is, there is this kind of ego-connect that inflates, even in worship, when everybody's hands are lifted or if everybody is jumping. You can't help but feel good about what you are doing.

But, to me, that is the bait! If you take the bait, well, you are already in danger.

I can't come into the King's courts and be concerned with the people along the way. If the King is one hundred feet in front of me and I am there to entertain Him, I can't go to all the people in the court and ask them what they'd like to hear, or see if they liked my lyrics. There's only the one thing the jester was concerned with—the King's face. Was he pleased, or not?

Back in the sixties and seventies, during the heyday of Johnny Carson and *The Tonight Show*, when a comedian would appear, all he or she was concerned with was what Johnny thought about it. It could absolutely make your career in one night if Johnny laughed. It could mean a potential sitcom if he called you over to his couch afterward. These entertainers knew that if Johnny liked you, you were "in." Jerry Seinfeld has talked about the first night he ever did *The Tonight Show*. He heard Johnny laugh, and in that instant he knew that his life would never be the same. The very next day he was in meetings with NBC about a weekly show.

That's the picture. When God sees your worship and likes something about you and your authenticity, He says, "Come over here and sit with Me." And suddenly, that's when life changes for all the Davids. David had brothers who were stronger, taller, and more experienced. David was out in a field with the sheep. Nobody was thinking about him. But there's the question of the heart. David was content to do what he was supposed to do. Nobody told him to go out and play a harp and sing to his sheep while he tended to them. But he did it because that was what he was created to do.

I like that. So, I have decided that I am going to play my guitar and sing to the sheep. Because it is then that I am singing to my King. And out of that comes this incredible access to the deeper things of God.

Worship Is HOT

As I mentioned earlier, the Christian music industry is now experiencing a tremendous influx of musicians flocking to worship. Why? Because it sells. Worship CDs used to be relegated to a little shelf in the back of the music display. But today, they are big business. And because of that, I'm afraid it is attracting some musicians who are primarily into their music and simply see worship as "the next hot thing." They are using their celebrity status to make something happen in the worship world.

But then there are other people, the obscure ones who are just leading their sheep—fellow jesters who are playing for the King. They are leading worship before congregations of 600, 400, or maybe only 100. They are in Rockford, Illinois, and Edina, Minnesota, and Wichita, Kansas. They stand up front and say, "God, all I want is You. All I want is to see You smiling."

That's the deeper level of worship. That's what my heart aims for each and every time I get up to lead worship. That's the picture I see. I know that I am in danger if I ever stop seeing that picture. Whenever I get to thinking that I have something to do with this, it is time to do some serious retooling. Every time I think they are looking at me, I need to refocus my gaze on the King.

A Conversation

I would never presume to define the totality of what worship is. To me, that would seem to be the height of arrogance. But I can tell you what true worship is for me.

A conversation between friends.

This definition has only come together for me in the last few years. Truth be told, for a long time, I had a hard time seeing God as a *friend*. I saw Him more as this tyrant, sitting in heaven judging me. Many of us have a distorted view of God because we've been influenced by people, sermons, or churches in our background that twisted the truth. The difference came when I finally realized that I was created for worship. It is the reason I was made. Then, everything changed.

Today, I am at my happiest and am most peaceful when I am drawing from what is inside of me, then hearing what the Lord says in return. That is the conversation. And, for me, that is worship. The beauty is, we all can have our own individual conversations with Him.

Jennifer Houghton
An Invitation to Holiness

In drawing closer to God, we must be in daily communication with Him. It is in our daily worship and reflection of His holiness, grace, mercy, and goodness that we gain an understanding of what it means to be like Him. It is in those intimate moments that we begin to tap in to God's heartbeat. As we continue to seek after His heart, He reveals sin in our lives that we may have never dealt with before. What better way to deal with those issues than in the presence of the Most High God?

When we daily give Him praise, we begin to capture His heart and develop an understanding of who He is. Then He will begin to impart all that He is into our hearts—His goodness, His mercy, His grace, His patience, His purity, His compassion, His love, and His holiness. As we begin to understand what it means to *"be holy as He is holy"* (1 Peter 1:15–16) and the more we worship Him, the more we will truly see His holiness and the more we will be made holy, setting us apart as a New Breed.

A DEEPER WORSHIP

Do you see the give-and-take there? Well, lucky for us, we do a lot more of the taking. I think that even people who are not musical, folks who don't feel comfortable singing, can relate to being in a conversation. Too many people see worship as merely the singing of songs. Churches have fed this notion because that's how they treat worship. We stop our service and say, "Okay, now we are going to worship." And we go into song time before we get to the more "important stuff" like the sermon or the offering. As a worship leader, I am often part of worship services where someone comes up to me and says, "Okay, here's the program. You have thirteen minutes to worship." Thirteen minutes to lead people into the presence of God and then it's over. Thanks for coming. Bye-bye. That thirteen-minute music set can be a part of worship, but it shouldn't be "the whole ball of wax."

Stacey Joseph
God Is God

A DEEPER WORSHIP

As I go through this consecration, I have realized that God has not talked to me as much as I thought He would. He has been silent a lot. That has been hard for me.

I can't even say that there has been this overwhelming sense of God's presence. There haven't been a lot of touchy-feely moments. The silent part is hard because you're focused and moving forward in this journey thinking, *God, You should be talking more*. You expect to discover incredible revelations and new spiritual truths. But He doesn't necessarily talk in the way that you would expect.

What I have become deeply aware of is more of a "God consciousness"—an acknowledgement that God is God whether I feel Him or not. My relationship with Him cannot be based on feelings or emotions. Few deep and intimate relationships are based on such things.

A part of maturing as believers is being faithful to Him, even when it appears that He is silent, or when we feel that He is not near. We must worship Him in the day-to-day, and not just on the mountaintop.

A Lifestyle of Worship

Stacey's journal is very typical. We often do this bargaining thing with God where we dedicate ourselves to Him through service, devotion, or by singing "worship songs," and then we feel that He now "owes" us something. We expect the deep, velvety voice of God to grace us with great wisdom as payback for all or our devotion.

Or, we might equate worship with tingly, emotion-packed moments that happen once in a blue moon. We imagine worship as something that can only happen with the right music, the right scenery, and the right feelings.

So, perhaps we should start by stating what worship is not:

- Worship is not a genre or style of music.
- Worship is not a fifteen-minute prelude to the Sunday service.
- Worship is not something to get a crowd warmed up.
- Worship is not a slow song—that's a ballad. (And, by the way, praise is not an upbeat song—that's an upbeat song.)
- Worship is not a transition.
- Worship is not even music!

So then, what is it?

Worship is a lifestyle.

To really go deeper, we must become worshippers. And to really become worshippers we have to get our minds out of the

Sunday morning service. We have to see our lives in God in their entirety—not just the moments we spend in a sanctuary or auditorium. You were created to make the praise of God glorious. Everything you do returns praise back to God.

Some of the greatest moments of worship I have ever experienced were when there was absolutely nobody around. It was in that little kitchen having this tangible conversation where I felt the presence of God. I heard Him speaking. I heard Him singing. Sometimes I like to imagine the change that would come to us if we could approach worship in that way.

If your heart is in the right place, you are living a life of worship to the Lord. It doesn't have to be singing or anything musical. In fact, usually it's not. It's my wife preparing my son's lunch for school. That's worship. It's the mom driving her kids to soccer practice in the afternoon. That, too, is worship. It's a mom or dad working diligently at a job forty hours a week to provide for the family. That's worship. It's living and worshipping and serving God with your life—every moment of the day.

Once you can look at worship as this lifestyle with God, it will take the whole idea of music out of the picture. And, speaking as a musician, I believe that needs to happen. Because if worship is merely a "music thing," then it becomes something that you move in and out of. During a service, I may sit back and appreciate the talent of those up front—maybe I'm moved and I clap or shout or tear up, but it stays tied to the music. Because of that, it is doomed to end as soon as the music stops.

Worship is a preparedness, not so much out of obligation, but because it is my reasonable service and gratitude to God for the fact that I am standing up. I have all my limbs. I have life. I have breath. I am healthy. I have the opportunity to nourish my son, take my kids to their events, and to provide for my family. Even if you're not healthy, you are called to worship, still grateful for what God has done and who He is. We don't worship only in those moments when we feel good and everything is going our way.

Even in our most mundane moments, it is a miracle that we are even here. And it is in that moment, with a heart of gratitude, that worship takes place. We stop taking the gifts of life, and family, and all God has blessed us with, for granted.

Describe a time when you experienced truly deep worship.

What was unique about it? How were you different?

A DEEPER WORSHIP

Think of a way in which you worship God in a completely nonmusical context.

What would have to change in your life for you to have a lifestyle of worship?

CHAPTER SIX

GOD'S CONSTANT PRESENCE

Open your mouth and taste, open your
*   eyes and see—how good GOD is.*
Blessed are you who run to him.
Worship GOD if you want the best; worship
*   opens doors to all his goodness.*
Young lions on the prowl get hungry, but
*   GOD-seekers are full of GOD.*

Is anyone crying for help? GOD is listening,
*   ready to rescue you.*
If your heart is broken, you'll find GOD right
*   there; if you're kicked in the gut, he'll*
*   help you catch your breath.*
*   —Psalm 34:8–10, 17–18 (MESSAGE)*

Several years ago, one of my heroes, worship leader Kent Henry, asked me a question: "Is it possible to constantly live in the presence of God?"

My answer was neither strong nor sure, because, truthfully, I didn't think it was possible. I believed, as many of us do, that falling into sin, tolerating habits, and carrying the weight of our humanness were just a part of this journey in Christ.

He suggested I check out the writings of a seventeenth century monk named Brother Lawrence. In his book, *The Practice of the Presence of God*, Brother Lawrence wrote several letters. This one is the last letter he wrote just a week before he died. I think it's incredible.

> Let us occupy ourselves entirely in knowing God. The more we know Him, the more we will desire to know Him. As love increases with knowledge, the more we know God, the more we will truly love Him. We will learn to love Him equally in times of distress or in times of great joy.

> Although we seek and love God because of the blessings He has given us or for those He may give us in the future, let's not stop there. These blessings, as great as they are, will never carry us as near to Him as a simple act of faith does in a time of need or trouble.

> Let us look to God with these eyes of faith. He is within us; we don't need to seek Him elsewhere. We have only ourselves to blame if we turn from God, occupying ourselves instead with the trifles of life. In His patience, the Lord endures our weaknesses. Even so, just think of the price we pay by being separated from His presence!

> Once and for all, let us begin to be His entirely. May we banish from our hearts and souls all that does not

reflect Jesus. Let's ask Him for the grace to do this, so that He alone might rule in our hearts.

I must confide in you, my dear friend, that I hope, in His grace, that I will see Him in a few days. Let's pray to Him for one another.[1]

Most of Brother Lawrence's life was devoted to walking in an intimate daily relationship with Jesus, and he proved that whatever you prioritize you will become obsessed with.

The Way of Intimacy

In the fall of 1970, my mother, a seventeen-year-old white girl, became pregnant by a young black man in Waterloo, Iowa. This was not even a decade removed from the Civil Rights struggles of the sixties. Let's just say that racial segregation was still deeply entrenched in American culture at that time.

When my mother went to her family, their advice was "have an abortion and get on with your life." After all, she was an accomplished concert pianist and had her whole life ahead of her. For some reason, though, she was determined to keep this baby. Her family shunned her, causing her to move to California.

Eventually, she ended up all alone, eighteen hundred miles from home. The state of California took her baby away and declared her an unfit mother because of the drugs in her system.

God knew what was going on, however, and led a woman to come up to my mother, completely out of the blue, and say,

[1] Brother Lawrence, *The Practice of the Presence of God* (New Kensington, PA: Whitaker House), 55–56.

"I don't know you, but I was driving by and I really felt that I needed to come tell you Jesus loves you. You're not forgotten. You did the right thing. It's going to be all right."

Those words of life were so powerful that my mother got on her knees on that San Diego street corner and gave her life to the Lord. I'm here today because of that woman's faithfulness to God to share the gospel with my mother.

When I was seven, I met my grandfather, the man who told my mother to abort her baby and move on. I saw other children from the family running up to him and jumping on his lap. It looked like fun. So I ran up and tried the same thing. But, unable to get over our racial difference, he pushed me back. The next thing I knew, I was lying on the ground, looking up and wondering, *What's wrong with me?* Eventually we were reconciled, but I'm not sure he was ever able to accept our differences.

Years later, it was again my friend Kent Henry who, during worship, said, "Just crawl up into your Father's lap and let Him love you."

As you might imagine, I had a problem with that.

Since then, I have found many other people whose view of God has been skewed by people in their past. It could be a parent or authority figure who abused their responsibility. It can be a Sunday school teacher who only taught a partial picture of God. Whatever it is, often the image we have of our heavenly Father is distorted, like one of those weird carnival mirrors. It overemphasizes some parts and de-emphasizes others, leaving us with a faulty and dysfunctional picture of just who God is.

Neville Diedericks,
Vocalist
Hometown:
Cape Town, South Africa
I Am Accepted

In many ways, I was always taught to be afraid of God. Not a reverential fear, but that fear that if you did something wrong, you should expect something bad to happen because of it. Because I was afraid of God, I tried to be perfect so He would accept me. Acceptance was a big deal for me, coming from South Africa and being black. But I could never get it right. And because I never got it right, I spent much of my life afraid of God and trying to please Him in my own strength.

It was years before the eyes of my heart were opened to see that there was nothing I could do to make God accept me. I finally realized that, in Jesus, I am the righteousness of God. And, because of that, I AM accepted.

We are not loved because we are perfect, but rather, we are perfect because we are loved.

We don't have to do anything to be righteous, but rather, we do right because we are made righteous.

Claim these truths today and ask God to change you at the heart level. I have found that it is much easier to change the outside once you have changed the inside.

GOD'S CONSTANT PRESENCE

Just think of how much time and opportunity is wasted because of our incomplete or just plain false view of God.

But God can use the negative experiences from our past for our good in the present. Through all of this I have realized that God was teaching me something important. He was saying,

I've seen you through all of this not to hurt you but to shape you, to be acquainted with the pain that a lot of people feel.

For me, diving into the Father's love and constant presence, and encouraging others to do the same, has been about not trivializing the pain that a lot of people who come to church are feeling, but helping them break through into what God really has for them.

For you created my inmost being; you knit me together in my mother's womb. I praise you because I am fearfully and wonderfully made; your works are wonderful, I know that full well. My frame was not hidden from you when I was made in the secret place. When I was woven together in the depths of the earth, your eyes saw my unformed body. All the days ordained for me were written in your book before one of them came to be.

(Psalm 139:13–16)

For so long, I bought into the belief that I was here accidentally—that I was a mistake. But the more time I have spent in God's presence, the more I have come to understand the truth of that psalm. I didn't just sneak into this earth; I was created for a purpose. When you come to live in the comforting, encouraging presence of God on a daily basis, it builds your confidence and faith in who He has made you to be.

It is just so obvious to me that we haven't even scratched the surface of what is available for us within the constant presence of God. Recently, Don Wilkinson had his view of God expanded.

A DEEPER LEVEL

Don Wilkinson
Hometown:
Springfield, MA
Ever Increasing Power

Several weeks ago, my wife, Steph, and I were on the road. We were having an ordinary conversation, nothing too deep, and then, out of the blue, she hit me with a question that rocked my world: "Do you feel you have power?"

As a man, I was thinking, *Of course I have power! What do you think this is?* Steph specified things further, "Not physical power, but supernatural power." That changed the entire dynamic of the question—and of my answer.

So I ask you, Do you feel like you have power?

When you pray, do you feel as if it is done?

How do I move mountains? I do it by faith. How do I get faith? Scripture says, *"Faith comes by hearing, and hearing by the word of God"* (Romans 10:17, NKJV). How does my faith move mountains? It moves them when put into action. James 2:17 says, *"Faith by itself, if it is not accompanied by action, is dead."* Faith in action gives you power.

In Matthew, the disciples were unable to heal a young boy, and Jesus said it was *"because you have so little faith. I tell you the truth, if you have faith as small as a mustard seed, you can say to*

> *this mountain, 'Move from here to there' and it will move. Nothing will be impossible for you"* (Matthew 17:20).
>
> It is imperative that we who are called to a deeper level not only understand the power that we possess, but that we also know and believe that we have the ability to change lives, impact nations, and affect future generations. Imagine if we could all identify and tap into that power—there would be no mountain we couldn't move!

That inspires me to continue to increase my prayer, devotion, and worship lifestyle; to eat healthy and exercise regularly; and to spend more time entertaining the King rather then myself. My desire is to ever live in the presence of the Lord. So, I ask you the same question asked of me twelve years ago:

Is it possible to constantly live in the presence of God?

Let's be found trying.

Are you living in the constant presence of God?

If not, why not?

What are some things you believe about God that come more from your past than from Scripture?

What does Scripture say to refute those things?

Deeper

Lord, I reach for You
Lead me to Your heart
And I thirst for You
Draw me deeper still
Deeper into the water
Deeper until I'm under

Oh, oh, living water flow and overtake us
Oh, flow
Healing water flow and overtake us
Close enough to feel the cadence of Your
*   heart*
Streams of justice flow to the least of
*   these*
Deeper into the water

God, give us a heart
Give us a heart
Give us Your heart
God, give us a heart
Deep cries out to deep
God, give us a heart
God, give us Your heart
God, give us a heart
For the least of these

CHAPTER SEVEN

WORSHIP AND JUSTICE

*I can't stand your religious
        meetings.
I'm fed up with your conferences
        and conventions.
I want nothing to do with
        your religion projects, your
        pretentious slogans and goals.
I'm sick of your fund-raising
        schemes, your public relations
        and image making.
I've had all I can take of your noisy
        ego-music. When was the last
        time you sang to me?
Do you know what I want?
        I want justice—oceans of it.
            I want fairness—rivers of it.
That's what I want.
                    That's all I want.*
                    —Amos 5:21–24 (MESSAGE)

magine being in the midst of the greatest worship you've ever experienced. The music is awesome. Your soul is soaring. Everyone is crying out to God. And then, in a quiet moment, the voice of God comes over the PA reading the Scripture above.

That is what has been happening to me over the past few months. I can hear the heart of God quoting those verses so clearly within my spirit. It is to the point that I am starting to believe that it is impossible to call myself a worshipper of God, someone who is close to the cadence and heartbeat of Jesus, and not be moved toward social justice.

Where's the Church?

I feel the weight of responsibility in this matter. I feel that any of us who have been given any kind of platform of influence in this world have no choice but to use what God has given us to make a difference—a significant difference—in the lives of widows, orphans, and the elderly.

It was a bittersweet epiphany when I saw Bono, the lead singer of U2, introduce his latest social effort, "Product Red." This is a licensed brand that he created with such companies as American Express, Apple Computer, Converse, Motorola, The Gap, and Giorgio Armani. Each company has created a product that carries the Product Red logo and gives a percentage of the proceeds to fight AIDS, tuberculosis, and malaria. In announcing the effort, he said, "Product Red is a result of us seeing a problem and forcing consumers worldwide to do something about it."

Later, in an interview with Bill Hybels, he said, "We are doing this because the church of America has not. She's still asleep!"

When I heard this, I felt angry and hurt because I knew he was right.

Therefore, I restate my claim that it is impossible to call ourselves worshippers, or worship leaders, and not be moved—even consumed—with God's heart for justice, compassion, and effective change toward "the least of these" around our community and around the globe.

I refuse to do another concert, or have another great gathering of believers, and not do my best to rally us as the body of Christ to consistent, authentic justice and measurable change.

The Stirring of Change

For me, this began around 1994 when I started to make visits to Africa once or twice every year. In 2005, we released a live worship CD that was recorded in Cape Town. The people there have always captivated me. When we play there, I see the radiance of the faces of these people who literally walk miles to hear us play. I know their feet hurt. I know that they are either going to walk back or cram onto a bus with a bunch of other people in order to return to a home that is nothing close to our American standard of a house. It is probably constructed of tin and has no air conditioning or even running water. And yet I watch them in worship, saying, "Jesus, I love You. You're the greatest!" It's amazing.

At some point, I decided that I couldn't experience all of that and then go back to Houston and lose it within a week. I was moved, and I tried to figure out why. I kept feeling God's heart so close. It wasn't about me feeling bad for being affluent or American. I think it was simply God showing me that these were people I liked hanging out with. But He was saying, "If you want to hang out with Me at a deeper level, you're going to have to tap into this."

Lanre Agbabiaka
God's Heartbeat

This consecration was intended to get us closer to God, to hear the heartbeat of God. And in hearing God's heart and passion, you begin to see that it is for people. *"For God so loved the world that he gave his one and only Son"* (John 3:16).

Therefore, if God's heart is for people, then my heart should be for people, too. And if worship is about putting God first, then obviously you are putting the heart of God first in your life.

So, if my heart should be about people, then the question becomes, What can I do to begin to really invest in people's lives and bring about what God sees for them?

The Least of These

Not too long ago, I felt myself in this moment of worship, and I was saying all the right things: "God, You're here. We just sense Your presence. Blah, blah, blah."

And I truly heard God say, "Dude, I'm not even here."

That tripped me up because there is nothing theologically correct about it. Obviously God is omnipresent—ever present, everywhere. And I certainly don't think that God goes around calling people "Dude." I just know what I heard. Afterward, I was confused. I asked God what it was about. It became a kind of challenge—an adventure. God was challenging me to seek what He was really all about. My friend and the spiritual leader of New Breed, Bishop Joseph Garlington, once defined justice as "apprehending the disposition of God's heart toward the broken."

That led me into Scripture, where I saw the kind of people Jesus was drawn to, and conversely, the people who got under His skin. I was really struck by His words in one particular passage of Scripture in Matthew:

> *"I was hungry and you gave me something to eat, I was thirsty and you gave me something to drink, I was a stranger and you invited me in, I needed clothes and you clothed me, I was sick and you looked after me, I was in prison and you came to visit me."*
> *Then the righteous will answer him, "Lord, when did we see you hungry and feed you,*

or thirsty and give you something to drink? When did we see you a stranger and invite you in, or needing clothes and clothe you? When did we see you sick or in prison and go to visit you?"

The King will reply, "I tell you the truth, whatever you did for one of the least of these brothers of mine, you did for me." (Matthew 25:35–40)

It has become clear to me that, according to this passage, Jesus not only cares for the poor and the broken; He identifies with them. He is with them, and they are a part of Him. They are one and the same. Where you find them, you will find Him!

The Lightbulb Moment

When I read that, a lightbulb went on.

In going deeper, we've been fasting and praying and getting in the Word—but these things are not an end in and of themselves. Fasting is not the centerpiece. Praying is not the destination. They take us somewhere deeper. Finally, we draw near to that heartbeat, and we are able to hear from God and know what is important to Him.

It should strike us as significant when an icon in entertainment like Bono says, "This is the paramount reason why I do what I do." We should take notice when Oprah says, "I was born to build this school in South Africa." She's worth a billion dollars. Why does that move her so?

God is the God of the universe. Sometimes God will say something to the church, but the church doesn't hear it. So God will use IBM; God will use Apple; God will use Bill Gates, or Bono, or Madonna. God doesn't care who it is; He will use whatever is at His disposal that His purposes will be accomplished on the earth. In the Old Testament, God made a donkey talk to save a man's life. (See Numbers 22.)

The church sees this and stands up and says, "Wow, we ought to be doing that." Bono basically stuck his finger in the face of the church and said, "What are you doing about it?"

The church's response is normally, "Well, who are you? You're a rock star. What do you promote?"

But Bono says, "I'm doing this because the church won't."

When people say things like that, I get provoked, because when you're talking about the church, it's like you're talking about my mama. But I realized he was right.

That's why we're saying that worship is a natural progression toward justice. Worship and touching the broken go hand in hand.

When we sing, "I want to be more like You, Jesus," or "Draw me nearer, blessed Lord, to You," I believe God answers by saying, "All right, come on. But when you realize who hangs out within My heart, you're going to be astonished, because they don't smell good, and they may not look right. They are not the people you would hire on your church staff. But these are the people that I really like being around. This is where you will find Me."

When he accepted the Chairman's Award from the NAACP, Bono said,

> The one thing we can all agree, all faiths, all ideologies, is that God is with the vulnerable and the poor. God is in the slums, in the cardboard boxes where the poor play house; God is in the silence of a mother who has infected her child with a virus that will end both their lives; God is in the cries heard under the rubble of war; God is in the debris of wasted opportunity and lives; and, God is with us if we are with them.[1]

A DEEPER LEVEL

---

[1] Bulluck, V. (Executive Producer). (2007, March 2). *38th NAACP Image Awards.* Los Angeles, CA: Vicangelo Films.

Lois Du Plessis
It Starts at Home

Being a part of this consecration and of this discussion about justice has made me want to go back to my church in South Africa. A lot of people who go to my church don't have anything. They don't have food to eat. One lady and her daughter come to church every week. She doesn't always understand everything, but they sit down in the front. Sometimes she sits there and holds her Bible upside down—but she comes.

This time of going deeper has made me think about those little things. Of going back to those hurting people and showing them that God cares about them, that they're important to Him.

Sometimes church can become about something as trivial as the glamour of what we are going to wear to church. Many of the people in my church don't have a choice. That lady and her daughter wear the same dress every week and sit in the same spot.

For me, going deeper is about going back there to make a difference in the lives of those people. To touch their lives with the love of God.

Blessed to Be a Blessing

I am often asked, "What do you think is next in worship? Where's it going?"

I hesitate to answer because with this deluge of music and worship and marketing, it can be hard to tell exactly where it's all going. And the truth is, it is easy to get frustrated with the whole Christian marketing scene—me, me, me; money, money, money; look at everything we've got!

But just when I am ready to cut off that particular nose to spite that particular face, I hear God saying, "You know what? I can use all this."

Really? But what about the influx of prosperity preaching? You know, the type of preaching that promises, "Just ask the Lord and you're going to get it. Just believe for that house, that car, all those blessings. He wants you to have them!"

Sometimes we treat God's Word as if it is such a delicate and fragile thing, that the least bit of doctrinal diversion will shatter the effectiveness of the Gospel. The truth is, the Gospel is resilient. It has survived for thousands of years through all kinds of heresy and church strife. The apostle Paul recognized this when discussing "false teachers:"

> *It is true that some preach Christ out of envy and rivalry, but others out of goodwill. The latter do so in love....The former preach Christ out of selfish ambition....But what does it matter? The important thing is that in every way, whether from false motives or true, Christ is preached. And because of this I rejoice.*
>
> (Philippians 1:15–18)

What Paul is basically saying is that God can use it all for the kingdom's purpose. Maybe it all comes back to this: perhaps we are blessed to be a blessing. That's the key. So, even with all this talk about how God wants you rich, maybe God can use that, too.

The next big question is, Why? Why are we blessed? The reason we are blessed is to be a blessing. Maybe that is the only thing that needs to be adjusted. Maybe what needs clarification is not the blessing, but for whom the blessing is intended. Who are you blessing?

Remember, when God made His covenant with Abraham, He did not do it just so that Abraham would become a chosen race. There was a greater purpose. God said, *"In your seed all the nations of the earth shall be blessed"* (Genesis 22:18 NKJV). All the nations of the earth would be blessed.

I recently saw an interview with pastor and author Rick Warren on CNN. He was asked if he thought it was a sin to be wealthy. Rick's response: "No. I think it's a sin to *die* wealthy." Rick was merely communicating what we've been told about money all our lives: you can't take it with you. We know that, but do we live like that?

It's like playing the board game Monopoly. You get all that funny-colored money to use in the game. But when the game is over, the money will do you no good. The money stays in the box. That's how it is for us. The resources that we are blessed with are to be put to work here. We are blessed to be a blessing—to all nations.

What's Next?

What's next in worship?

I think we are going to find that the closer you get in real worship—in true worship, not the whole music industry scene, but the closer you get to God's heart—the more you will understand what He is all about. Then we will realize that the reason He needs you to be wealthy is not to buy another house in Vail, or another jet ski, or another Escalade. Perhaps the reason He needs you to be wealthy is to find where there is true despair, true hurt, true lack, true need—and meet it. Period.

We are blessed to be a blessing.

Suddenly, I have a different reaction. I'm not as bothered by all this new attention paid to worship. I'm not as bothered by all this prosperity talk. Sure, I think some of it has been abused and completely twists Scripture, but if people are able to get out of debt and save and invest, now they have the ability to do something. Now God can use them.

And when it is coupled with worship, when it's brought together with a heart of gratitude for what God has done, then we start realizing that God is truly moving us to be His hands and feet.

That's what's next: more people entering into a lifestyle of worship where they are blessed to be a blessing. And I began to realize that that's where God is. That's living in the constant presence of God.

God is with the migrant farm worker living in a Central American hut.

God is with the baby dying of AIDS in Africa.

God is with the leper on the streets of India.

God is with the guy on the freeway exit by my home with a sign that says, "Will work for food."

I know what you're thinking, But I've been burned by guys like that! And that's the challenge. To get past the paralyzing feeling of doing nothing, roll up our sleeves and say, "Okay, I have this money. What now?"

That's why the world appreciates people like Warren Buffett and Bill Gates, who are some of the greatest contributors to charities and world causes. They're showing us that you can have it all, but what matters is what you do with it.

I believe it is necessary for the church to start realizing her purpose and start meeting the needs that truly exist out there. I want to be one of those who cry, "Come on, let's do it together!"

When you think about it, it's really a natural progression, because worship is a conduit that moves our praise and attitude toward God. In doing so, we become people with hearts of gratitude. Even the Bible says you can't praise if you're not thankful. And that leads us to get out of the church and look around and see the hurting and needy, both next door and around the world. It all comes back to gratitude.

I believe that's what God is just beginning to do within His church. It happens when the church starts mobilizing and says, "Together, all of us who call ourselves Christians and tithers, if we all truly desired to bless the poor and needy, we could make a radical difference on this earth."

I think it began with the Asian tsunami and continued through the crisis caused by Hurricane Katrina. It all caused the church to step up and decide that we were going to be among the ones helping out there.

It hasn't gone unnoticed. Several of the relief agencies, like FEMA and the Red Cross, have said, "The churches, have really stepped up." What a blessing it is to divert the notion that some people have of the church being strictly out for people's money.

Lanre Agbabiaka
The Next Generation

Becoming a part of World Vision has been so important, because it has made me ask, "What am I doing? What am I doing to reach the forgotten? How am I going to impact those people we pass by every day?"

I've even thought about the next generation. Too often we look at the teenagers and we stereotype them to be this or that. As parents, we kind of overlook them because they don't act like us and they don't do what we do.

As a result, we shy away from them. We overlook them. We count them as nothing when they are often crying out as much as the homeless, as much as the hurting. They need God just as much.

I was so proud when the church where I lead worship, Lakewood Church in Houston, Texas, donated an entire weekend offering—over $1 million—to the victims of Hurricane Katrina. Rick Warren, author of *The Purpose Driven Life*®, donates the vast majority of his book proceeds to fight AIDS and hunger.

I'm ready for this to continue and ignite. I'm ready for this next move to be a move of generosity, a move of compassion and giving in world service. That's what I am looking forward to.

I am waiting desperately to see the church shine. I am at this point where I can sit around and complain and make a great argument for what's wrong, or I can take that same energy and start making a difference, even a small difference. I want to use whatever voice I have to help bring that about.

Justice Begins in Your Pew

We need to take Lanre's example to heart. Justice is not just about Africa or Indonesia or the third world. Obviously, that's a big place of need. But there are people sitting in our churches, or in our neighborhoods, who are as bankrupt in spirit as anyone. There are other kinds of poverty besides economic poverty. There are people suffering from relational poverty, emotional poverty, spiritual poverty—justice can start in the pew of your church.

There's someone there who feels abandoned and orphaned. In that moment of worship, when you are connecting with God and hearing His heart for the wounded and broken—start right where you are. Find the broken among you.

There you will find Jesus.

Welcome to the deeper level.

What are the world needs that stir your heart?

What are the needs within your own community that stir your heart?

If you don't know, how can you find out?

An Invitation

World Vision is an international Christian relief and development organization whose stated goal is "working for the well being of all people, especially children." Working on six continents, World Vision is one of the largest Christian relief and development organizations in the world. Each member of New Breed has committed to financially sponsor a child through this organization.

For just thirty dollars a month, about a dollar a day, sponsors help to provide the basics that every child needs—clean drinking water, food, health care, and the chance to learn to read and write.

We invite you to join us in this venture. Please visit our website at www.newbreedmusic.com and click on the link to World Vision.

Say So

What does it mean to be saved
Is it more than just a prayer to pray
More than just a way to heaven
What does it mean to be His
To be formed in His likeness
Know that we have a purpose

To be salt and light in the world
In the world
To be salt and light in the world

Let the redeemed of the Lord say so
Let the redeemed of the Lord say so
Let the redeemed of the Lord say so

Oh that the church would arise
Oh that we would see with Jesus' eyes
We could show the world heaven
Show what it means to be His
To be formed in His likeness
Show them they have a purpose

Let the redeemed of the Lord say so
Let the redeemed of the Lord say so
Let the redeemed of the Lord say so

—by Michael Gungor and Israel Houghton

LYRICS

CHAPTER EIGHT

Saying "Yes" to God

Joshua said, "You are witnesses against
yourselves that you have chosen to serve
the LORD."
"**Yes**, we are witnesses," they replied.
"Now then," said Joshua, "throw away the
foreign gods that are among you and
yield your hearts to the LORD, the God of
Israel."
And the people said to Joshua, "We will
serve the LORD our God and obey him."
—Joshua 24:22–24 (emphasis added)

When New Breed was in Nigeria, I asked my friend
from South Africa Lionel Peterson to pray for us
before we went on stage. He agreed to pray, but
first he said he heard us talking about the deeper level. He said,
"The deeper level is when you just walk in it. Miracles, signs,
and wonders need to simply happen. You're going to walk in it.
That's the deeper level."

You see, the calling of God is not about how talented you
are. The movement of God's Spirit is not about how compelling

the sermon was or whether you "connected" with the music that day. It's about the change that happens in people's lives. It's when growths and cancers and tumors fall off or wither away. It's when people are released from addictions. It's when marriages are restored. It's when broken, hurting people come to the foot of the cross and fall into the embrace of a loving God.

Israel Houghton is not in this just to make a living playing music. New Breed is not coming together just to be a musical group. We want to make a difference in our society and culture.

Is that in your heart?

Ryan Edgar, Vocalist
Hometown: Charleston, SC
Working It Out

"Dear children, let us not love with words or tongue but with actions and in truth" (1 John 3:18). The apostle John reminds us that showing real love, love that is alive, awake, and moving, is how God desires for us to exist. In action, this means that we need to be ready for the works that He has prepared for us do. Be ready to serve people, look for ways to bless others, even when there will be no reward for it. Let's collectively move in the direction of loving more, and we will experience His deep and abiding presence. We will go to a deeper level collectively by loving from a deeper level personally.

What if, like Esther, we've all been put here *"for such a time as this"* (Esther 4:14)!

What If?

We are here because of the *What if?*

Forty years ago, a revolution began. It started in the sixties but then went into the church and became what was known as the Jesus Movement, where my mother was saved.

- *What if* I'm here today as a product of that generation's salvation?
- *What if* I'm here at thirty-five years old because I'm supposed to be a part of a new revolution?
- *What if* you're supposed to play a part in it as well?

That's a pretty big calling to consider. Frankly, I'm not sure I want that kind of responsibility. I already have enough going on in my life. So why do I keep coming back to this? Why am I pushing in on this?

Can you relate? Have you ever wondered if there might be more to this Christian life than just going to church on Sunday, maybe again in the middle of the week, and trying to maintain some kind of a quiet time? Do you ever wonder if God is calling you to something more than putting in a few hours serving somewhere in the church? There's nothing wrong with any of that—it's wonderful. But could there be more?

Is there more to this thing that Jesus talked about when He said, *"Repent, for the kingdom of heaven is near"* (Matthew 4:17)?

As we said earlier, going deeper means caring about the things that God cares about. It means putting aside our desires and plans and allowing God to implant His desires in our hearts.

Now, going deeper means that I am far more concerned about the things of God than the things of Israel Houghton. Suddenly you start saying the things that He is saying; you start thinking the things that He is thinking. Then, before you know it, you don't have to set aside your desires anymore, because the things of God have become your things.

"Get To" instead of "Got To"

Too many people are going to church saying, "What can I get out of Sunday? I better get blessed today. I better get something out of this today."

How many times have you been in a position of saying, "I've *got* to go to a worship service tonight." Or, "I've *got* to sing in the choir tonight."

I've *got* to.

We all do that. After a while, it becomes an obligation.

I found myself doing that. One day, I was driving to church when somebody called and invited me to an Astros game. I grimaced and said, "Aw, I can't. I've *got* to lead worship tonight."

Almost immediately, I heard the Lord say, "Excuse Me?" It surprised me. It was almost like someone was in the backseat.

God clearly said, "You've *got* to? There was a time you saw this as a 'get to,' not a 'got to.'"

And I remembered a time when "get to" came just as easily as "got to" came to me in that car.

I thought back on those early days and returned again to my first love. I remembered when I couldn't wait to get back in that kitchen. I remembered the things I said when I didn't know quite so much:

"Guess what? I *get to* play in the praise band tonight!"

"I *get to* lead worship at the midweek service!"

What happened along the way? Can you relate to this? Can you remember what turned your *"get to"* into *"got to"*?

"They hurt me."

"They turned my mic down."

"They said my skirt was too short."

"I don't like the alto I'm standing next to."

I hung up the phone that day and drove with tears coming down my face, saying, "Oh, Lord, I am so sorry. I don't know how I got to this place." I didn't know how it happened, but I had lost sight of the fact that leading God's people in worship is a privilege.

Not Our Concierge

There are still times when I don't feel it. I go to pray, and there's no revelation. I read God's Word, and it just seems like words on a page. But even in those times when I'm in need, I have enough sense of protocol to know that I can't treat God like a concierge. The concierge is the employee of a hotel whose job is to get the guests whatever they desire. If they need dinner reservations, show tickets, transportation, or whatever, the concierge is the person to see. But that is not God.

We've all been in that place where we come into God's presence, saying, "Lord, give me this. Heal that. Bless me. Give me. It's still not done. What's the delay, Lord?"

I've certainly been guilty of that. Thank God, I have learned that when I come into His presence, saying, "Lord, You are holy. You are faithful. You are powerful. You are just. You are sufficient for me," I can rest in Him. I can get quiet and begin to let Him speak to me.

There is a story of a famous preacher who met a king in the Middle East. He was given only twenty minutes to spend with the king. When they met, the preacher spent the first eighteen minutes telling the king of his own exploits. The king didn't say a word until the famous preacher was done. Then the king said, "I'm sorry that you used all your time telling me something that I already knew." And with that, their time was done. This preacher was in the king's presence. If he would have just shut up, he could have possibly gained wisdom or influence by being in the king's presence.

We can spend our time in God's presence in a similar way. Our time is limited, so we spew out our list to Him: "My son, fix him. My daughter, fix her. My boss, fix him. My husband, good Lord, fix him!" But we can miss the whole privilege of why we are there in the first place.

If you go to the President of the United States, even if you didn't vote for him, you know you don't just start speaking when he comes in the room. There is an order. He will speak first. There is a protocol. The greatest in the room speaks first.

The funny thing is, we treat God like He doesn't see what we need. Do you realize that before you even go to God, He knows what you need? He's not in heaven saying, "You're kidding! She needs what? Where are My angels? Why didn't you tell Me? She has a need down there and nobody told Me!" God knew what you needed when He woke you up this morning. So I've started praising Him the moment I come into His presence. I exhaust every word I know that would describe Him.

My daughter taught me this. She had heard me talking about God already knowing our needs before we ask, and then she came to me one day as I got off the phone.

I asked her, "Are you okay?"

"Yeah, Daddy, I'm fine. I just woke up this morning and was thinking about how you work so hard, and you're so strong, and I know sometimes you go away, but it's because you provide for us. And you're so great, and so smart, and so talented, and you're the greatest dad in the world. And I love you, not just for what you do, but just because you're my daddy."

By the time she was halfway done, I had the keys in my hand. We went to Target and Toys "R" Us. She was telling me what I wanted to be, what I know I am. I am the greatest dad in the world. "Get in the car, let me show you!"

The amazing thing is, and as hard as it is for me to admit, as much as I love my daughter, our heavenly Father loves us even more!

Getting to the "Yes!"

Meleasa and I have been married now for thirteen years. But in the beginning, every morning as I would wake up, I would turn to her and say, "I'm sorry."

"You're sorry?" she would say. "What for?"

I would reply, "I don't know. But at some point today, I just know I'm going to need to cash that in."

When Bishop Garlington heard this story, he liked it so much that he adopted it and adapted it. He gave it a little twist and wondered, "What if we woke up every morning and just said 'Yes!' to God?"

"Yes?" God would say. "Yes to what?"

And we would answer, "I don't know. But at some point today, You're going to ask me to serve You and I want to cash that in right now."

Do you realize that, at any time, Jesus could suddenly decide, "I think I want to be the most popular thing on earth right now. Who can I trust to carry that?"

He's God. Everything in the world is His. MTV is His. Sony Music is His. They may not know it; they may not acknowledge it, but *"the world is* [His], *and all that is in it"* (Psalm 50:12). Every bit of commerce, entertainment, government—everything is His.

- *What if* God just decides, "I want it all back...the captains of industry, the politicians, the artists, and the influencers"?
- *What if* Angelina Jolie starts declaring that Jesus is Lord?
- *What if* Tiger Woods starts declaring that Jesus is Lord?

- *What if* David Letterman starts declaring that Jesus is Lord?
- *What if* North Korean leader Kim Jong-il starts declaring that Jesus is Lord?
- *What if* it starts with you and me?

To a great extent, the deeper is getting to that "Yes!" It is saying, "God, You breathed life into me so many years ago. You established a certain framework and DNA inside of me. Now, You want it back. You have a plan for it. And I just want to say 'Yes!' to that."

What if we start saying "Yes!" to the things of God. "Yes!" to the heart of God? "Yes!" to the discipline of God? "Yes!" to the pain and the fellowship of suffering with God? Just say "Yes!" no matter what the ultimate outcome is.

Bono says he believes that we can end extreme poverty in this generation. That is an incredible statement when you look at it. But I look at that and say, "Yes!" It may be a lot for a rock star to say, but it is nothing for God.

- *What if* the church of Jesus Christ decided that we were going to get serious about living for Him?
- *What if* we went deeper into making His desires our desires?
- *What if* we clothed the naked, fed the hungry, visited the prisoners, and cared for the sick and broken?
- *What if* the kingdom of heaven came near?

I believe this is a generation that can walk in that calling.

Throughout this consecration, what do you find yourself saying "Yes!" to?

What is a dream that God has put on your heart that is so big you are afraid to tell anyone?

* Photographs by ColemanArt Photography (www.ColemanArtPhotography.com)

About the Author

I srael Houghton has garnered acclaim as one of Christian and Gospel music's foremost worship leaders, songwriters, recording artists, and producers. Engaged in full-time ministry since 1989, Israel has touched the hearts of millions across the globe through his anointed, God-inspired music.

In 1995, Israel and Meleasa Houghton founded New Breed Ministries, an organization comprised of noted musicians and singers who serve within their respective churches and together serve the Church at large.

With a desire to draw people of all races, ages, and cultures together through worship, Israel and New Breed began melding sounds and songs to create music that breaks down barriers and defies categorization. Not an easy task, but it seems effortless for Israel, who laughingly describes himself as "a black kid who grew up in a white family in a Hispanic neighborhood."

Together with the vocalists and musicians of New Breed, Israel uses his own multi-cultural upbringing as a reference point. "It's not a white sound or black sound, it's a Kingdom sound," explains the songwriter and producer.

Although their popularity had been growing steadily since the group's inception, they were catapulted into the limelight during 2005 with the release of their gold-certified CD, *Live From Another Level.* They followed this success with two others—the release of the gold-certified *Alive in South Africa* in late 2005 and *A Timeless Christmas* released in the fall of 2006. The accolades continued to flow, including multiple Dove Awards and Stellar Awards, a Soul Train Award, and a Grammy Award. The group has also made numerous appearances at high-visibility events including the *The Stellar Awards* and *The Dove Awards* presentation shows, as well as BET's *Lift Every Voice* and *Celebration of Gospel*, TBN's *Praise The Lord*, and CBN's *The 700 Club*, to name a few.

All the while, this dedicated group of ministers tours extensively and pursues serving at their local churches. But, even with such busy schedules, Israel and New Breed have recorded two more CDs—*Sound of the New Breed: Freedom*, a studio album currently in stores, and their newest project, *A Deeper Level*, a live CD that released in September '07.

Israel continues to serve as a worship leader at Houston's Lakewood Church. He and Meleasa make their home near Houston with their three young children.

Additional information about
Israel and New Breed is available at:
www.NewBreedMusic.com
www.IntegrityGospel.com/ADeeperLevel

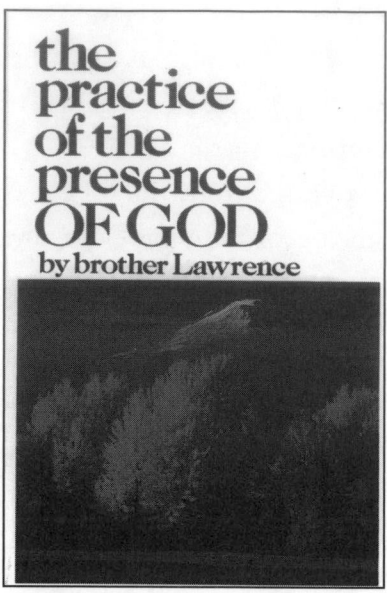

The Practice of the Presence of God
Brother Lawrence

Brother Lawrence was a man of humble beginnings who discovered the secret of living moment by moment with a sense of God's presence. It is the art of "practicing the presence of God in one single act that does not end." For nearly three hundred years, this unparalleled classic has given both blessing and instruction to millions who can be content with nothing less than knowing God in all His majesty and experiencing His loving presence throughout each day.

ISBN: 978-0-88368-105-3 • Paperback • 96 pages

WHITAKER
HOUSE

www.whitakerhouse.com